Greek and Roman Sport

Greek and Roman Sport

*A Dictionary of Athletes
and Events from the
Eighth Century* B.C. *to
the Third Century* A.D.

by
David Matz

McFarland & Company, Inc., Publishers
Jefferson, North Carolina, and London

The author is grateful to Harvard University Press for permission to use the following material:

Page 7. Pausanias, 5.10.1. Reprinted by permission of The Loeb Classical Library from Pausanias: *Description of Greece*, Vols. II and III, W. H. S. Jones, translator, Cambridge, Mass.: Harvard University Press, 1926, 1933.

Page 40. Pausanias, 6.4.6. Reprinted by permission of The Loeb Classical Library from Pausanias: *Description of Greece*, Vols. II and III, W. H. S. Jones, translator, Cambridge, Mass.: Harvard University Press, 1926, 1933.

Page 95. Athenaeus 10.412E. Reprinted by permission of The Loeb Classical Library from Athenaeus: *The Deipnosophists*, Vol. IV, Charles Buron Gulick, translator, Cambridge, Mass.: Harvard University Press, 1930.

Pages 107–108. Dio Cassius 73.19,22. Reprinted by permission of The Loeb Classical Library from Dio Cassius: *Roman History*, Vol. IX, Earnest Cary, translator, Cambridge, Mass.: Harvard University Press, 1927.

Pages 110–112. Sidonius Apollinaris *To Consentius* 23.317–427. Reprinted by permission of The Loeb Classical Library from Sidonius: *Poems*, Vol. I, W. B. Anderson, translator, Cambridge, Mass.: Harvard University Press, 1936.

Pages 112–114. Dio Chrysostom, excerpts. Reprinted by permission of The Loeb Classical Library from Dio Chrysostom: *Discourses*, Vol. II, J. W. Cohoon, translator, Cambridge, Mass.: Harvard University Press, 1939.

British Library Cataloguing-in-Publication data are available

Library of Congress Cataloguing-in-Publication Data

Matz, David.
    Greek and Roman sport : a dictionary of athletes and events from the eighth century B.C. to the third century A.D. / by David Matz.
        p.   cm.
    Includes bibliographical references (p.   ).
    ISBN 0-89950-558-9 (55# alk. paper : lib. bdg.) ∞
    1. Sports – Greece – Dictionaries.   2. Sports – Rome – Dictionaries.
3. Athletes – Greece – Biography – Dictionaries.   4. Athletes – Rome – Biography – Dictionaries.   I. Title.
GV17.M38   1991
796'.03 – dc20   90-53509
                                                                                  CIP

Manufactured in the United States of America

McFarland & Company, Inc., Publishers
    Box 611, Jefferson, North Carolina 28640

Contents

v

Preface

In the long history of classical scholarship, no one has heretofore compiled a reference book containing descriptions of the terms and events of Greek and Roman sport, and information about the athletes who excelled in those events. This book is intended to supply that information.

The book has been organized into the following eight parts:

1. A Brief History of Greek and Roman Sport
2. Sources (ancient and modern)
3. The Dictionary
4. Special Essays (various topics discussed at more length than individual biographies allow)
5. Lists of Athletes and Horses (from various ancient sources)
6. Classical Texts Cited (a list of ancient sources furnishing information which appears in the biographical entries)
7. A Glossary of Places (including each place of origin cited in the athletes' biographies)
8. An Index

Literally hundreds of names of Greek and Roman athletes are known. Some of these competitors, such as the Greek wrestler Milo of Croton, are well attested, with clear and full accounts of their achievements in the ancient sources. Many others, however, are little more than names attached to particular events.

The biographies of the athletes in the Dictionary range in length from several lines to several paragraphs. In no instance should the amount of space devoted to an athlete give rise to inferences about his prominence in his event or his time period. The quantity of the primary source material dictates to a large extent the length of an individual's biographical sketch.

Some readers may expect more detailed chronological informa-

1

tion than this book provides, but there is in many instances none to offer. Whenever possible, the dates of an athlete's career are provided, but frequently, precise or even approximate dates cannot be determined. The athletes included in this book date from as early as the eighth century B.C. to as late as the third century A.D.

Semilegendary athletes such as those described in Homeric epic have been omitted. The earliest known athlete included in the book, the stade racer Coroebus, flourished in the eighth century B.C.

Some of the stories of the athletes' exploits may seem apocryphal. For the most part, no attempt has been made to assess the validity of these stories. Nor has there been an effort to identify or explain elements in the biographical information that may have been allegorical or metaphorical. Evaluations of these kinds are best left to the reader.

For the convenience of those readers who may not be thoroughly familiar with the idiosyncratic method used by classicists for citing ancient authors, the full name of each author has always been written in full. (Example: Pausanias, not Paus.) If more than one work is associated with an author, the (English) title of that work has also been written in full. (Example: Plutarch *Life of Alexander*, not Plut. *Alex.*)

Some writers, most notably Pausanias, produced but one extant work. In those cases, only the citations have been provided, without the title. (Example: Pausanias 6.15.1, not Pausanias *Description of Greece* 6.15.1.) The authors to whom this particularly pertains:

> Athenaeus (whose only extant work is *The Learned Banquet*)
> Dio Cassius *Roman History*
> Dio Chrysostom *Orations*
> Diodorus Siculus *World History*
> Diogenes Laertius *Lives and Opinions of Philosophers*
> Dionysius of Halicarnassus *Roman Antiquities*
> Eusebius *Chronology*
> Herodotus *Histories*
> Juvenal *Satires*
> Martial *Epigrams;* when *Concerning Spectacles* is meant, that
> title will appear
> Pausanias *Description of Greece*
> Philostratus *On Gymnastics;* when the *Life of Apollonius* or
> the *Images* is meant, that title will appear

Pliny the Elder *Natural History*
Thucydides *The Peloponnesian War*

Finally, references to the victor list are to Eusebius, who adopted it from the original compiler, Sextus Julius Africanus. The Eusebian list is bilingual; references are to odd-numbered column numbers (the Latin version), as published in Schoene's edition of Eusebius' *Chronology.*

The abbreviation *q.v.* following an athlete's name means that a separate biography of that individual appears in the Dictionary.

All dates are B.C. unless otherwise noted.

There are perhaps sections of this book that the serious scholar will find unnecessarily didactic. For example, a reader who already knows the location of Scotussa or Acragas, Dyme or Astypalaea, would probably be advised to pay no note to the Glossary of Places. Likewise, one who has committed to memory the names of the Pindaric athletes might wish to avoid the listing of same in Part V. It was my intention that this book should provide a wide selection of facts and information, readily available and clearly indicated, so as to enable users to obtain quickly the material they need, while allowing them to disregard that which they already know.

In their prefaces, the authors of nonfiction books frequently pay homage to the many scholars and teachers who have assisted them in the composition of their manuscripts; at the same time, they admit the impossibility of assigning proper credit due every source for every fact and idea that may appear in their books. While I have endeavored to credit my sources as fully and as copiously as possible, I would reserve for myself the right of "innocent infringement" in places where facts and ideas may lack adequate attribution.

List of Abbreviations of Sources

Information on these and other sources may be found in Part II; this list is provided for ease of reference.

AEspA: *Archivo Español Arqueología*
CIL: *Corpus Inscriptionum Latinarum*
FGH: Felix Jacoby, *Fragmente der griechischen Historiker*
IAG: Luigi Moretti, *Iscrizioni agonistiche greche*
IG: *Inscriptiones Graecae*
ILS: Hermann Dessau, *Inscriptiones Latinae Selectae*
Syll³: Wilhelm Dittenberger, *Sylloge inscriptionum Graecarum*, 3rd ed. 1915-1924

I. A Brief History
of Greek and Roman Sport

Greek Athletics

No one knows why the ancient Greeks began celebrating a quadrennial athletic festival at the otherwise unassuming plain in the northwestern Peloponnesus Greece called Olympia. Nor can anyone state with confidence the name(s) of the founder(s) of the games. Nor is it known exactly when the games were founded, although the first date for which there are official records, 776 B.C., is traditionally considered the inaugural year.

According to Pausanias, who is one of our most informative sources on the history and development of the Olympic games, the only event in the first Olympiad — and in the twelve to follow — was the stade race. Other contests were gradually added, including the diaulos (in 724), the dolichos (720), the pentathlon and wrestling (708), boxing (688), four-horse chariot racing (680), the pankration and horse racing (648). Hence, by the middle of the seventh century, most of the principal events were on the Olympic program; after that time, few adjustments to the schedule were deemed necessary.

Events for boys aged 18 years and under were instituted at the 37th Olympiad (632); prizes were offered in the foot races and wrestling, and later in boxing (616) and in the pankration (200). A boys' pentathlon was added in 628, but was immediately discontinued, for reasons that remain unclear.

The entire festival was compressed into a span of five days. The first and last days were reserved for ceremonies and celebrations both religious and secular. The order of the contests in the middle three days is uncertain, but it appears that the equestrian events and the pentathlon occurred on the second day, the boys' events on the third, and the remainder — boxing, wrestling, the pankration, the foot races — on the fourth.

5

The games were administered by the residents of the nearby town of Elis. Not surprisingly, Elis could point to a disproportionate number of its native sons attaining Olympic glory; presumably, these athletes had ready access to the facilities at Olympia throughout the year, giving them a decided edge over contestants from other parts of the Greek world, many of whom undoubtedly had never even seen Olympia until the first time they competed there.

In addition to furnishing the presiding magistrates *(agonothetes)* of the games, the Eleans also supplied the judges *(Hellanodicae)*. Originally, only one judge was deemed necessary. However, as the numbers of events and participants increased, so did the need for *Hellanodicae*. Two judges were appointed to work the 50th Olympiad (580); by 400, their ranks had grown to nine: three to oversee the chariot racing, three the pentathlon, and three for the remaining events. By the 108th Olympiad (348), ten judges supervised the games; that number apparently remained constant until the demise of the Olympics.

Prospective Olympians were expected to arrive in Elis 30 days prior to the start of the competitions, apparently to give the administrators and judges time to determine their eligibility. Background and age checks had to be conducted on those wishing to enter the boys' events. Preliminary heats needed to be run in order to reduce the fields for each of the contests to a workable number. Finally, there were oaths to be taken; each athlete was required to swear that he would not violate any of the regulations of the games, and that he had trained for ten successive months in preparation for his one day of competition.

Oath and rule breakers usually received substantial fines. Among the infractions: offering or accepting bribes; cowardice in boxing or the pankration; failing to observe the 30-day arrival deadline; attempting to arrange grudge matches. Additionally, representing a city other than one's own, while perhaps not technically a rules violation, often brought severe punishment to athletes who engaged in the practice.

Although champions received only an olive wreath at Olympia, their hometowns often treated them to far more valuable rewards, including cash, free board and other amenities. Furthermore, many of the less prestigious athletic festivals — and there were hundreds annually — offered money or goods and commodities as prizes to the winners. Hence, successful athletes could amass fortunes. The well-known heavy eventer Theagenes of Thasos was once assessed a fine of two talents by the authorities at Elis for breaking the rule against grudge matches; he apparently had little difficulty in liquidating the debt. (While the dollar equivalency of a talent is difficult to gauge, some idea of its value may be gained by considering that 6,000 Greek drachmas equalled one talent, and that the annual salary of an average Greek worker probably did not exceed 1,000 drachmas.)

Of the prestige and importance of the Olympic games, there can be no doubt. They attracted spectators and athletes from every corner of the Greek world. Time was measured in Olympiads, with 776 as the starting point. The games went on every four years without fail for over a millennium; neither war, nor famine, nor geopolitics could quash them. Pausanias captured their essence succinctly: "Many are the sights to be seen in Greece, and many are the wonders to be heard; but on nothing does Heaven bestow more care than on the Eleusinian rites and the Olympic games." (5.10.1.) (Loeb Classical Library translation.)

Roman Athletics

Greek-style athletic festivals never found a wide audience among the Romans. The men of the Tiber favored above all two spectator sports far removed in conception and execution from the groves of Olympia: chariot racing and gladiatorial shows.

CHARIOT RACING. Chariot races, the *ludi circenses*, occupied an important place in Roman life almost from the time of the city's founding in 753. According to the historian Livy, Romulus (Rome's founder and first king) instituted chariot racing at Rome. Livy also asserts that another legendary king, Tarquinius Superbus, first designated the site of Rome's great race course, the Circus Maximus. The narrowness of the valley (between the Palatine and Aventine Hills) where the Circus was located limited to twelve the number of chariots that could race there at one time; however, the lower slopes of the hills provided convenient accommodation for a great number of spectators. Originally, the Circus may have seated 150,000 people; after subsequent additions (most notably by Julius Caesar), its seating capacity may have reached upwards of 250,000.

The long (over a quarter mile) and narrow race track was bisected for much of its length by a low dividing wall usually referred to as the *spina* (although according to Humphrey in *Roman Cir-cuses*, the standard term in antiquity was *euripus*); a typical race consisted of seven circuits around the *spina*. The hairpin turns at either end precluded the attainment of high speeds on the straight-aways, and also demanded of the drivers the utmost in judgment and finesse; negotiating the turns too sharply could cause a chariot to roll, while swinging too widely would result in the driver losing any favorable positioning he may have gained on the straightaways.

Once the race began, the charioteers were permittted great lati-tude in their efforts to win. Crowding an opponent, blocking his path, or causing him to crash were all legal tactics. The ability and willingness of a driver to force a rival to lose control of his team was clearly a sine qua non for success in the highly competitive world of Roman chariot racing.

Even without pressure from an opponent, it was no small mat-ter to exercise mastery over the horses — typically four to a chariot — used in the races. Specially bred for service on the track, they were strong, muscular, high-spirited creatures, bending only to the will of the most skilled and experienced drivers. To aid in controlling the horses, charioteers customarily looped the slack of the reins around their waists for added leverage. The obvious disadvantage of this practice came into play if the chariot overturned during the race. Unless a driver who found himself in that precarious situation could extricate himself quickly from the tangle of reins, he faced the un-pleasant prospect of being dragged along behind the chariot, in-evitably suffering serious, perhaps fatal, injuries.

Charioteers in Rome were grouped into teams known as fac-tions *(factiones)*. Factions were official organizations of racing com-panies whose responsibility it was to provide horses, chariots, drivers and equipment for the games. Originally, there were but two factions, the White *(factio alba, or albata)*, and the Red *(factio russata)*. Later — presumably in the first century A.D. — two more factions emerged, the Green *(factio prasina)* and the Blue *(factio veneta)*.

That drivers could and did switch factions is indisputable. Many, in fact, drove for all four factions at one time or another in their careers. Whether such transfers were initiated by the drivers or by faction management is unknown. Nor is it known whether drivers were bound by contractual agreements, or whether they were the original free agents, who could search for the most profit-able terms of employment.

What is certain, however, is that the most proficient charioteers could become wealthy. The second century A.D. driver Appuleius Diocles, for example, earned in excess of 35,000,000 sesterces over the course of his 24-year career. As in the case of talents (see above), no attempt will be made here to provide a dollar equivalency for that sum; however, some idea of its value may be gained by considering that the emperor Augustus established a property requirement of 400,000 sesterces for Rome's thriving merchant class, the equestrians. It may be assumed, therefore, that any Roman with a net worth of 400,000 sesterces or more enjoyed a comfortable, if not affluent, lifestyle. Whether drivers were permitted to keep all their winnings is a matter of some conjecture, but even if they retained only half, it would be in many instances a substantial amount — over 17,000,000 sesterces in Diocles' case.

The factions inspired fierce loyalty and generated unbridled enthusiasm among the crowds that flocked to the Circus Maximus to view the races. Even some of the emperors got into the act. Vitellius (ruled A.D. 69) and Domitian (81–96) were fans of the Blues, while Caligula (37–41) and Nero (54–68) supported the Greens.

The popularity of the factions (particularly the Blues and the Greens) extended beyond their imperial devotees and affected the commoners as well. The satirist Juvenal noted sarcastically that if a Green faction driver should lose, the fans of the *factio prasina* would be as depressed and dismayed as the city had been the day the Romans lost the Battle of Cannae (216 B.C.) — one of the most humiliating and decisive defeats in Roman history.

Under the Roman Republic, the games of the Circus were provided as public entertainment by politicians eager to court popular favor. The responsibility for financing the races fell especially to first-time seekers of office, the ones who might be the most anxious to establish name recognition among the voters. Under the Empire, the Circus games continued to be presented by these magistrates since by that time, sponsoring races had become a traditional duty of their offices. However, the emperor might also assume this role in order to amuse the commoners and to keep them content. Juvenal, caustic as ever, observed in his well-turned phrase that the lower classes of Roman society cared for nothing but *panem et circenses*, bread and circuses.

Chariot races were held in conjunction with annual festivals and holidays. The most prominent of these were the Ludi Megalenses (April 3–10); the Ludi Cereales (April 12–19); the Ludi

Florales (April 28–May 3); the Ludi Apollinares (July 6–13); the Ludi Victoriae Caesaris (July 20–30); the Ludi Romani (September 4–19); the Ludi Victoriae Sullae (October 26–November 1); and the Ludi Plebei (November 4–17). Chariot races occurred only on specified days of each festival. (For additional information about the origins, dates and events of these and other holidays, see Friedlaender [Vol. II, 11–12] or Balsdon [245–248].)

GLADIATORIAL SHOWS (MUNERA). The Roman institution of gladiatorial shows evolved from a model borrowed from the Etruscans, though there is some evidence of a more general Mediterranean origin. The earliest known gladiatorial show presented in Rome was produced during the consulship of Appius Claudius and Marcus Fulvius in 264 B.C. Its sponsor was a certain Decimus Junius Brutus; the occasion was the death of Brutus' father. The somewhat modest total of three pairs of gladiators performed.

After that time, the custom of exhibiting gladiators in concert with funeral rites gradually became more common; in 216, the three sons of Marcus Aemilius Lepidus gave funeral games lasting for three days and utilizing the talents of 22 pairs of gladiators. Sixteen years later, 25 pairs fought in the forum as part of the funeral ceremony for Marcus Valerius Laevinius; his sons Publius and Marcus sponsored the show. Similar performances, but on an increasingly lavish scale, occurred in 183 at the funeral of Publius Licinius; in 174 at the funeral of Titus Flamininus; and in about 145 at the funeral of the grandfather of Gaius Terentius Lucanus. The connection with funeral rites was weakened when, in 105, the consuls Publius Rutilius Rufus and Gaius Manlius gave the first official gladiatorial games.

The gradual but unmistakable shift of *munera* from funerary to secular occasions apparently continued over the course of the next thirty years, with the result that the shows became institutionalized, replete with training schools and stables of professional gladiators. In 73 a serious rebellion of slaves and gladiators under Spartacus broke out, and it was not until more than two years later that the full force of Roman military strength was able to corral Spartacus and crush the revolt.

The uprising of Spartacus revealed to the Romans in a most bitter and powerful manner that high concentrations of gladiators could result in volatile situations inimicable to Roman interests. Therefore, although private individuals were allowed to own gladiators, some legal restrictions were applied to those individuals. For example, in his aedileship of 65, Julius Caesar produced a gladiatorial show, but with restrictions on the number of participants.

It had gradually become customary in the late Republic for lower echelon office holders and seekers of office to put on gladiatorial shows (and to sponsor chariot races) as a means of attaining popularity. Therefore, laws were also passed to restrict the production of gladiatorial shows as a political ploy. The orator Marcus Tullius Cicero engineered a measure which made it illegal for political candidates, whether declared or prospective, to give *munera* within two years of the date that they actually ran for office.

After Augustus consolidated his position at the head of the Roman government, he enacted several reforms, including a prohibition on the producing of more than two shows per year, and an upper limit of 120 men participating in them. Despite these restrictions, Augustus claims in his autobiography to have sponsored eight shows in which about 10,000 men fought.

In imperial times, the production of lavish gladiatorial contests became increasingly the responsibility of the emperor or his close associates. Nearly all the emperors of the first century A.D. were involved in sponsoring the shows. And it was in that century that one of Rome's most famous landmarks, the Coliseum (called the Flavian Amphitheater in antiquity) was constructed.

Gladiatorial shows continued to be presented for centuries thereafter until the moral authority of Christianity began to make itself heard. At a *munus* in the early fifth century, a monk named Telemachus supposedly ran into the arena to try to put a stop to the proceedings; in the riot that ensued, he was dismembered by the crowd. Shortly afterwards, the emperor Honorius banished the games altogether.

Contrary to popular belief, gladiatorial ranks were not filled primarily by Christian conscripts. Rather, most gladiators were drawn from among slaves, criminals and prisoners of war. And a surprising number of free Roman citizens volunteered, undoubtedly lured by the same inducements that attract their modern counterparts into high-risk occupations like professional football or hockey: money, fame, love of competition, hordes of adoring admirers.

The notion that gladiatorial combat was a kill-or-be-killed affair is also erroneous. Owners of gladiators invested large amounts of time and money in the training of their charges; as businessmen, they clearly would not wish to see their resources — the gladiators — facing constant depletion. Also, many gladiators became famous, so much so that their names often appeared on posters advertising upcoming shows. The frequent demise of these "drawing cards" would surely have had a negative impact on attendance, another undesirable outcome from the perspective of the gladiatorial bureaucracy. It is therefore unlikely that the primary object of a gladiator was to kill or even seriously wound his opponent; rather, his aim seemed to have been only to force his adversary to admit defeat, in precisely the same manner in which Greek boxing and pankration matches were decided. For more explication of this contention, see Special Essay 6, pages 114–119.

II. Sources

Ancient Literary Sources

Scattered references to athletic competition occur in the works of many Greek and Roman writers. Several are singled out as having particular importance for the compilation of this dictionary.

Claudius Aelianus (Aelian; ca. A.D. 170–235). Aelian's chief extant works are two: *On Animals*, a series of stories set in the natural world, and *Various Histories*, a similar series dealing with humans. The latter is a particularly useful resource, containing a good deal of biographical information about many athletes. Unfortunately, there is at present no English translation of *Various Histories*.

Athenaeus (flourished ca. A.D. 200). Athenaeus' only extant work, *Deipnosophistae (The Learned Banquet)*, is an interesting and fast-paced narrative of the dinner table conversation of a number of philosophers and intellectuals. References to athletes and athletic competition occur with surprising frequency.

Dio Chrysostom (the "Golden-mouthed"; ca. A.D. 40–112). Dio was a Romanized Greek philosopher and orator who left some eighty extant speeches.

Diodorus Siculus (the "Sicilian"; flourished 1st century B.C.). Diodorus wrote a world history in 40 books, beginning with the earliest times and continuing to Caesar's Gallic War. Most of his references to Greek athletes are short; the Olympiad in which they won a crown is usually the extent of his interest in them, although occasionally he provides more detail.

Dionysius of Halicarnassus (late 1st century B.C.). Dionysius was an historian who wrote, among other works, *Roman Antiquities*, an account of Roman history from its beginnings to the time of the First Punic War (mid–3rd century B.C.).

Eusebius (ca. A.D. 260–340). The "man of many notebooks," Eusebius was a prolific early Christian writer. His best known work

13

is probably his *Church History*, but he also wrote a book entitled *Chronology*. Included in the latter is a list of all Olympic stade race winners from 776 B.C. to A.D. 217, based on a similar compilation by Sextus Julius Africanus.

Herodotus (ca. 490–425 B.C.). Called by some the "Father of History," Herodotus' historical account of the Persian Wars is supplemented by numerous stories and anecdotes, a few of which concern noted athletes.

Juvenal (ca. A.D. 50–120). A caustic and embittered satirist, Juvenal frequently castigates Roman society and morality within the pages of his 16 surviving *Satires*.

Lucian (2nd century A.D.). The possessor of a fertile and creative mind, Lucian was the author of some 80 short essays, on a wide variety of topics. Sports and athletes were among the topics that often captured his attention.

Martial (A.D. 40–110). A witty and sophisticated epigrammatist, Martial in his poems touches upon nearly every facet of Roman society; he did not neglect the shows and games within the pages of his writings.

Pausanias (2nd century A.D.). A writer of travelogues, Pausanias journeyed to the site of the Olympic Games and compiled a detailed account of their history, including information on hundreds of Olympic athletes. His work is the single most important source for biographical data about the competitors who won championships in the Olympiads of the sixth, fifth and fourth centuries.

Philostratus. There are four known writers bearing the name Philostratus, with occasional uncertainty over which extant writings should be attributed to which Philostratus. The work cited extensively in this dictionary, *On Gymnastics*, has been credited to the second of the four Philostrati (ca. A.D. 170–250); this training manual is the only one of its kind surviving from antiquity. Also assigned to this Philostratus: *Life of Apollonius*.

The third Philostratus (flourished 3rd century A.D.) is the presumed author of *Images*.

Pindar (518–438 B.C.). Pindar was the author of odes honoring victorious athletes (epinicean odes). Some 45 of his poems are extant. Many are fraught with abstruse imagery and unknown references, but the careful reader may learn a great deal about the Greek athletic establishment from a close examination of the Pindaric poems. Other important epinicean poets include Bacchylides (505–450 B.C.) and Simonides (556–467 B.C.).

Pliny the Elder (A.D. 23–79). Pliny wrote an exhaustive, 102-volume treatise on natural history, as well as a number of (now lost) historical, military and biographical works. He perished in the eruption of Mt. Vesuvius.

Plutarch (A.D. 46–120). The famous biographer and essayist was a tireless researcher and collector of information about many aspects of antiquity, including sport.

Suetonius (A.D. 70–140). Like Plutarch, a polymath biographer who provides incidental material about charioteers and gladiators within the pages of his writings about the Roman emperors. He also describes the athletic dabblings of emperors who would be gladiators or charioteers, especially Caligula and Nero.

Marcus Tullius Cicero (106–43 B.C.). The preeminent Roman orator of his time period, and one of the most gifted Latin prose writers of any time period, Cicero's many works provide a wealth of information about Roman political, military, philosophical and social history.

Xenophon (ca. 430–354 B.C.). Xenophon was a Greek historian and writer of over a dozen books and treatises on topics ranging from history and biography, to financial and property management, to horsemanship and hunting.

Other writers whose works were consulted in the preparation of this reference book include the philosophers Plato (428–347 B.C.) and Seneca (4 B.C.–A.D. 65); the philosopher and biographer Diogenes Laertius (3rd century A.D.); the orators Aeschines (4th century B.C.) and Demosthenes (384–322 B.C.); the comic playwrights Aristophanes (450–385 B.C.) and Menander (342–290 B.C.); the grammarian Quintilian (1st century A.D.); the geographers Solinus (3rd century A.D.) and Strabo (64 B.C.–A.D. 21); the poets Catullus (84–54 B.C.), Horace (65–8 B.C.), Lucilius (2nd century B.C., not to be confused with the 1st century A.D. epigrammatist Lucillius, whose extant poems are included in *The Greek Anthology*), Sidonius Apollinaris (5th century A.D.), Statius (A.D. 45–96) and Theocritus (3rd century B.C.); the essayist Aulus Gellius (A.D. 123–165); the novelist Petronius (died A.D. 65); the encyclopedists Pollux (2nd century A.D.) and Photius (820–891); the historians Arrian (2nd century A.D.), Dio Cassius (flourished 3rd century A.D.), Livy (59 B.C.–A.D. 17), and Phlegon (2nd century A.D.); Polybius (200–120 B.C.); and Thucydides (460–400 B.C.).

The poems and epigrams of a wide variety of Greek authors have been published in a collection called *The Greek Anthology*, the product of many compilers working over the course of nearly a millennium; it was finally complete by the 10th century. The compendium (also called the *Palatine Anthology* or *Anthologia Palatina*) has yielded a fair amount of information, often humorous, about Greek athletes. Fragmentary material from the writings of Greek historians, collected in Felix Jacoby's *Die Fragmente der griechischen Historiker*, has been cited as *FGH*.

Epigraphical Sources

Evidence from inscriptions is important for piecing together the picture of Greek athletics, crucially so for the Romans. Many collections of inscriptions have been published, usually annotated. The most comprehensive and useful of these are the *Corpus Inscriptionum Latinarum (CIL)* and the *Inscriptiones Graecae (IG)*. Particularly important for the history of Greek sport is Luigi Moretti's *Iscrizioni agonistiche greche (IAG)*, a collection – with commentary in Italian – of 90 inscriptions pertaining to Greek athletes. Valuable inscriptional material on Roman gladiators may be found in an article by Antonio García y Bellida, "Lápidas Funerarias de Gladiadores de Hispania," in *Archivo Español Arqueología (AEspA)* 33 (1960), pages 123–144. Other collections of inscriptions cited in this book include Hermann Dessau's *Inscriptiones Latinae Selectae (ILS)*, and Wilhelm Dittenberger's *Sylloge inscriptionum Graecarumm* 3rd ed. 1915–1924 (Syll³).

The inscriptions vary widely in form, content, length and complexity. Some are short, perhaps only a few lines or even a few words. Others continue for dozens of lines, providing a wealth of statistical and biographical data that no ancient writer (save perhaps Pausanias) would ever have considered including in a formal manuscript. Some inscriptions, such as epitaphs, are formulaic and generally understandable; others are packed with technical terms whose meanings can only be surmised; still others are fragmentary, with maddening lacunae at key points.

Given the variety of material contained in inscriptions, and the likelihood that archaeological excavations will yield new finds yearly, the importance of epigraphical evidence to the ancient sport historian can scarcely be underestimated. It would not be too rash to suggest that, in the case of Roman gladiators and charioteers, inscriptional evidence ranks ahead of literary sources in terms of the athletic detail it provides.

Archaeological Sources

Archaeological discoveries offer much of interest to the sport historian in addition to inscriptions. Discuses, runners' starting blocks, portions of chariots, bits and harnesses, and other items of equipment have been found. Stadia, hippodromes and gymnasia have been unearthed and reconstructed. Depictions of runners, wrestlers and boxers painted on vases provide glimpses of athletes in the heat of competition, as do their statues.

Modern Literary Sources

The study of ancient sport has experienced something of a renaissance in recent years, pushing to more than 1,000 the number of books, articles and monographs on the subject. Obviously, it would be neither possible nor appropriate to describe or even refer to all of these in the following bibliographical essay. I have attempted to include here the entries which I have found particularly useful and interesting. Readers may also wish to consult the bibliographies of Crowther or Scanlon (see below) for additional information.

Each year's scholarly work in classical studies is summarized in an ongoing series entitled *L'Année philologique*. A similar series, *L'Année epigraphique*, is devoted to the publication of recently discovered inscriptions. These two well-indexed sources should serve as the starting points for a serious attempt to compile a bibliography on any aspect of antiquity. General reference works in German *(Real-Encyclopaedie d. klassischen Altertumswissenschaft)*, French *(Dictionnaire des antiquités grecques et romaines)* and English *(Oxford Classical Dictionary)* offer useful articles.

The most recent and most inclusive bibliographical resource pertaining to sport in ancient Greece may be found in *Classical World* 78.5 (1985) and 79.2 (1985). This two-part series, "Studies in Greek Athletics" by Nigel Crowther, contains over 1,200 entries, many of them annotated. Regrettably, there is no comparable survey for Roman sport. Thomas Scanlon's *Greek and Roman Athletics: A Bibliography* (1984) is also useful.

Rachel Robinson's *Sources for the History of Greek Athletics* (1955) is a sound and readable collection of the most important primary source material on Greek sport. Another sourcebook, W. E.

Sweet's *Sport and Recreation in Ancient Greece* (1987), is aimed more at a student readership; its 33 chapters are replete with discussion questions. Again, however, no comparable manuals exist for the Roman side of the story.

E. N. Gardiner's *Athletics of the Ancient World* (1919), while outdated and sometimes insipidly idealistic, contains a number of useful illustrations and diagrams, as well as occasionally insightful treatments of the events and organization of Greek sport. Despite the broadness of purpose implied in the title, however, the reader will find little treatment of the Romans.

Ludwig Drees' *Olympia* (1967), a lavishly illustrated, copiously footnoted tome, is a sober and sound treatment of the subject, one which the specialist and general reader alike will find useful. Those who are interested in the material remains at Olympia should find Drees' book particularly beneficial.

Two well-researched books by Luigi Moretti are the previously mentioned *Iscrizioni agonistiche greche* (1953; cited as *IAG* in the biographies) and *Olympionikai: I vincitori negli antichi agoni olimpici* (1957). The latter is a compilation of the names of all known Olympic champions. Biographical and bibliographical data are always provided, sometimes in great profusion. As the titles suggest, both books are written in Italian. Unfortunately, Moretti's books (especially *Olympionikai*) seem to be in short supply, at least in the United States, and only the most well-stocked research libraries are likely to own copies.

A detailed and scholarly inquiry into the terminology of Greek wrestling, boxing and pankration may be found in Michael Poliakoff's *Studies in the Terminology of the Greek Combat Sports* (1982). Greekless readers will perhaps be frustrated by this heavily footnoted book's lack of English versions of the passages quoted at length from Greek authors. Poliakoff's second book, equally erudite and well written, but more geared to the nonspecialist, was published in 1987: *Combat Sports in the Ancient World*. As with Gardiner's *Athletics of the Ancient World,* however, the title is more inclusive than the contents; the author omits any substantive consideration of the Romans.

Donald Kyle's *Athletics in Ancient Athens* (1987) stands as the first detailed study of the subject. This scholarly work includes in one of its appendices the names of 116 known and possible Athenian athletes; each entry is accompanied by biographical and bibliographical information.

Of the many annotated translations of the Pindaric corpus, the best by far is Roy Swanson's *Pindar's Odes* (1974). Not only are the translations first rate, but the lengthy introduction contains a comprehensive and well-written account of the history and the events of the Olympic games.

J. G. Frazer's five-volume commentary on Pausanias contains numerous insightful comments and analyses. It is particularly beneficial to the reader who knows Greek, but Greekless readers will also use these volumes to their advantage.

The best English-language book on sport in ancient Greece is quite arguably H. A. Harris' *Greek Athletes and Athletics* (1964). More readable, more sober and more fully documented than Gardiner's effort, it serves as an excellent introduction to ancient Greek sport. Its companion volume, *Sport in Greece and Rome* (1972), contains the most useful discussion of Roman sport currently available (despite the omission of material on gladiators).

Two serviceable books which include chapters on Roman gladiators and charioteers are Ludwig Friedlaender's *Roman Life and Manners Under the Early Empire* (the English translation of the 7th edition [1909] of his monumental *Sittengeschichte Roms;* see especially Volumes II and IV) and J. P. V. D. Balsdon's *Life and Leisure in Ancient Rome* (1969). The latter is copiously documented.

Strangely, there are few English-language books on the two most popular spectator sports of the classical Roman world, chariot races and gladiatorial shows. Alan Cameron has written two books on the former, *Porphyrius the Charioteer* (1973) and *Circus Factions: Blues and Greens at Rome and Byzantium* (1976), but both of these treat the subject in the late Roman Empire. There is no detailed study of chariot racing centered upon earlier centuries in the city of Rome. John Humphrey's massive *Roman Circuses: Arenas for Chariot Racing* (1986), an exhaustive and thorough study of Roman racetracks, does not treat in detail charioteers, factions, racing strategies, and the like.

III. The Dictionary

Greek Athletes

In the entries for athletes, the following order has been observed: the athlete's name; his event(s); the approximate dates he flourished; his place of origin (usually but not necessarily his birthplace); his exploits; and a cursory bibliography of ancient sources. Many athletes are attested in only one or two ancient sources. Readers whose needs take them beyond the bibliographical citations provided in this book should consult Moretti (see *Modern Literary Sources* in previous chapter).

The phrase "Greek athlete" was applied to any competitor who hailed from a Greek city. Hence, Greek athletes came from places like the Greek colony of Croton (in southern Italy), and from Cycladic islands such as Thasos, and from Greek cities in Asia Minor such as Halicarnassus. One need not have been born and bred on mainland Greece to have been considered a Greek athlete.

It was customary for champion Olympic athletes to dedicate statues of themselves, with inscribed bases. The most skillful sculptors of the time were usually commissioned to construct the statues. Many of these sculptors' names are known; Pausanias records dozens of them. However, no information about the artists is included in the biographies of athletes, as it would seem to have no direct relevance to the task at hand. The reader whose interests lead him or her to seek more information about the sculptors or their works should consult Moretti, or W. W. Hyde's *Olympic Victor Monuments and Greek Athletic Art* (1921).

For the same reason — irrelevancy — no attempt has been made to include extraneous information about the athlete's hometown, although the hometowns represented have been listed alphabetically in the Glossary of Places.

20

A NOTE ON TRANSLITERATION. Maintaining consistency in transliterating from Greek to English is a desideratum not easily attained. I have attempted to adhere to the following system, with exceptions as noted:

Greek alpha-iota to "ae". Example: Heraea, not Heraia.

Greek epsilon-iota to "i". Example: Clitomachus, not Cleitomachus.

Greek kappa to "c". Example: Clitomachus, not Klitomachus. Exception: pankration, not pancration.

Greek nu-delta-rho-omicron-sigma to "nder". Example: Nicander, not Nicandros.

Greek omega-nu to "on". Example: Dicon, not Dico. Exception: Milo of Croton, whose name should be rendered "Milon," but who is so much more commonly known as "Milo" that I have retained that form.

Greek omicron-iota to "oe". Example: Coroebus, not Coroibus.

Greek omicron-upsilon to "u". Example: Butas, not Boutas.

Greek omicron-sigma to "us". Example: Clitomachus, not Clitomachos. Exception: certain place names, such as Andros, not Andrus.

Greek upsilon to "y". Example: Pyttalus, not Puttalus. Exception: the epsilon-upsilon diphthong, such as Eupolemus, not Eypolemus.

Every effort has been made to conform to these rules. Should the perspicacious reader notice an aberration, the author earnestly solicits his or her indulgence.

A NOTE ON INCLUSION CRITERIA. The best-attested athletes — Milo, Theagenes, Oebotas, Polydamas et al. — have been included not only because of their outstanding physical skills, but also because of the relative profusion of relevant primary source material. Athletes who performed notable "firsts" have found their way into these pages, e.g. the first man to win an Olympic championship in a particular event. Athletes who pioneered some innovative training method, dietary regimen or competitive stratagem appear here. On the more dubious side, malcontents, cheaters and bribe-takers also have their place in this book. While no claim is advanced that every Greek athlete known to modern scholarship is represented herein, most of the prominent, successful and interesting ones have been included.

Unless otherwise noted, all individuals credited as chariot racers and victors in equestrian events were the owners of the horses, not the drivers or riders. This usage follows the Greek tradition of awarding the crown of victory to the owner, not the driver or rider.

Chronologically, the list encompasses a period from the 8th century B.C. to the 3rd century A.D. Brackets enclosing the approximate date for an athlete indicate uncertainty about that date. In all cases, bracketed dates have been adopted from Moretti's chronology in his *Olympionikai*. (See *Modern Literary Sources* in the previous chapter.)

Roman Athletes

The Roman athletes are presented in a format similar to that utilized for their Greek counterparts: name, event, approximate dates, place of origin, exploits and sources.

When an athlete has more than one name (many Romans had bi- or tripartite names), the initial letter of his family name determines where his biography is placed. (This is the second name of a tripartite name.)

The overwhelming majority of Roman athletes were charioteers and gladiators. Very few were born in the city of Rome. Most were provincials who immigrated to the capital, where the opportunity for fame and wealth was the most propitious.

The emphasis is on gladiators and charioteers from the western half of the Roman empire. (The Byzantine period lies outside the scope of this book.)

For those individuals whose careers can be dated, the emphasis is on those who were active between the third century B.C. and the third century A.D.

The Dictionary Proper

A pompa. (Literal meaning: "from the procession.") A typical day of Roman chariot racing began with a ceremonial lap. It was apparently a special honor to win the first race after the procession; the designation *a pompa* (claimed by several drivers) seemed to have been applied to such a victory.

Acanthus. Greek dolichos racer, 8th century, Sparta. Acanthus won the dolichos in the 15th Olympiad (720), the first year in which the dolichos was an Olympic event. He may also have been the first man to compete nude. (See Orhippus). Sources: Dionysius of Halicarnassus 7.72; Eusebius 195; Pausanias 5.8.6; Philostratus 12.

Acilius Glabrio. Roman *bestiarius*, 1st century A.D., place of origin unknown. Glabrio rose to the consulship (A.D. 91) in Rome, but he also had a sort of second career, as a *bestiarius* in the arena. So great was his fighting skill that he was once ordered by the emperor Domitian to appear at the Juvenalian games, and there to kill a large lion. Glabrio adeptly slew the beast, escaping unharmed in the process. Domitian later used this incident, and Glabrio's addiction to beast fighting, as an excuse to have him executed. Sources: Dio Cassius 67.14; Juvenal 4.94–100.

Acmatidas. Greek pentathlete, late 6th century, Sparta. An inscribed jumping weight belonging to Acmatidas states that he won the pentathlon *akoniti.* Source: *IAG 8.*

Acusilaus. Greek boxer. *See* Diagoras.

Publius Aelius Gutta Calpurnianus. Roman charioteer, dates and place of origin unknown. Calpurnianus was a highly successful charioteer, employed by all four factions at various stages of his career. He won a total of 1,127 races: 102 for the Whites, 78 for the Reds, 583 for the Blues, and 364 for the Greens.

His 102 victories with the Whites included 83 in singles races, seven in doubles races and two in triples races. (There is no explanation for the discrepancy between 102 claimed total victories, and the sum of 83+7+2, 92.) Calpurnianus won one 30,000 sesterces race for the Whites, and one worth 40,000. He also recorded two *remissus* victories, and one victory with a horse that had never raced *(equus anagonus).*

Numbered among his 78 Red faction triumphs were 42 in singles races, 32 in doubles, three in triples and one in a four-team-mate race. He added one *remissus* victory while with the Reds, and one victory in a 30,000 sesterces race.

It was with the Blue and Green factions that Calpurnianus won the vast majority of his races; hence, the statistical information about his exploits with these two factions is more copious.

Of his 583 Blue faction victories, 334 came in singles races, 184 in doubles and 65 in triples. He won the 30,000 sesterces prize 17 times, the 40,000 sesterces prize nine times, including seven with three-horse teams, and the 50,000 sesterces prize eight times, including seven with three-horse teams. He also gained one victory each with a six-horse team, and with a horse that had never raced. Thirty-five of his 583 wins were post-processional.

Three horses with which he drove to 257 of his triumphs with the Blues were a black African named Germinator (92), a russet African called Silvanus (105), and a bay African named Nitidus (60).

His 364 Green faction victories included 116 in the singles, 184 in the doubles and 64 in the triples. He also recorded four 30,000 sesterces triumphs, four 40,000 sesterces wins, six post-processional victories and 61 on foot toward the chariot *(pedibus ad quadrigam)* during his stint with the Blues.

As a Green faction driver he drove most often (although not necessarily successfully) with the following horses: Danaus, a bay African (19 times); Oceanus, a black African (209); Victor, a russet African (429); Vindex, a bay African (157).

The lengthy inscription which provides this information concludes with the words *hoc monumentum vivus feci* ("I made this monument while alive"), suggesting that it may have been a plaque commissioned by Calpurnianus to commemorate his retirement. Source: *CIL* 6.10047. *See also* Harris' discussion in *Sport in Greece and Rome*, pages 203, 204, 205.

Aeschylus. Greek stade/hoplite racer, 5th century, place of origin unknown. Aeschylus won four stade championships and three hoplite championships in contests identified in his inscription as *damosioi;* the precise meaning is uncertain. Source: *IAG* 10.

Aeserninus. Roman gladiator. *See* Pacideianus.

Aesius Proculus (epithet *Colosseros*, "Big Cupid"). Roman gladiator, 1st century A.D., place of origin unknown. Aesius Proculus, son of a centurion, received his epithet by virtue of his imposing physique and handsome face. The emperor Caligula forced this unfortunate man to fight in the arena, first against a Thracian gladiator, then against a *hoplomachus*. When Proculus defeated both, Caligula ordered him to be tied up and dressed in rags, and then to be paraded through the streets of Rome and finally executed. Suetonius suggests that Caligula's boundless jealousy drove him to treat Proculus in this manner. SOURCE: Suetonius *Life of Caligula* 35.

Agenor. Greek boxer. *See* Eupolus.

Agesarchus. Greek boxer, [2nd century], Tritaea. Agesarchus won boxing championships at the Olympian, Nemean, Pythian and Isthmian festivals, presumably in succession although Pausanias does not specify this. SOURCE: Pausanias 6.12.8.

Ageus. Greek dolichos racer, 4th century, Argos. After winning the dolichos at the 113th Olympiad (328), Ageus ran home to Argos to announce in person the news of his triumph. He covered the distance—about 65 miles—in one day, the same day on which he had won at Olympia. SOURCE: Eusebius 205. A dolichos runner named Ageus also appears in the Lycaean victor list (*Syll*[3] 314; *see* Appendix), although it is not certain that he was the same man who won at Olympia in 328.

Agitator. The standard Latin word for charioteer, although *auriga* also occasionally appears in Roman terminology.

Agitator miliarius. An honorary title bestowed on a Roman charioteer who had won 1,000 (or more) races.

Aglaus. Greek stade/diaulos racer, 5th century, Athens. Aglaus won two foot racing crowns at the Isthmian games and two at the Nemean. He also competed successfully at Thebes, Pellana and Aegina. SOURCE: Bacchylides *Ode 9*.

Agonothetes. (Literal meaning: "contest placer," or "administrator.") A Greek term which referred to the magistrates who presided over the Olympic games.

Akoniti. (Literal meaning: "without dust.") At some Greek athletic festivals, especially less prestigious ones in small localities, a champion heavy eventer who had won at any of the crown festivals would so intimidate potential rivals that none dared face him. He would then win on forfeit, *akoniti*, without having to apply dust to his body (as heavy eventers commonly did prior to a match).

Albanus. Roman gladiator *(eques)*, dates and place of origin unknown. The inscription pertaining to Albanus says he was a graduate of the Ludus Magnus and he lived 22 years, 5 months, 8 days. He fought 11 times, but the text does not state the victory total. Source: *CIL* 6.10167.

Alcaenetus. Greek boxer, 5th century, Leprae. Alcaenetus won boxing championships in both the boys' and men's divisions at Olympia. His son Hellanicus won the boys' boxing at the 89th Olympiad (424), while his son Theantus duplicated that feat in the following Olympiad. Source: Pausanias 6.7.8.

Alcibiades. Greek chariot racer. *See* Special Essay 3, pages 105–106.

Alcimidas. Greek wrestler (boys'). *See* Praxidamas (II).

Alexander. Greek stade racer. *See* Crison.

Amabilis. Roman gladiator *(secutor)*, dates unknown, Dacia. Amabilis fought thirteen times. The laconic text of his inscription concludes with the words *fato deceptus non ab homine*, "taken in [i.e. killed] by fate, not by a man." Source: *CIL* 3.14644.

Amandus. Roman gladiator (Thracian), dates and place of origin unknown. Amandus, a graduate of the Ludus Nerionianus (a training school in Capua), participated in 16 bouts before his death at the age of 22. Source: *AespA* 33 (p. 128).

Amertes. Greek wrestler, [5th century], Elis. Amertes won a crown in boys' wrestling at Olympia, and later triumphed in the same event in the men's division at the Pythian games. Source: Pausanias 6.8.1.

Androleus. Greek boxer, dates and place of origin unknown. Androleus lamented that he had lost an ear at Olympia and an eye at Plataea, so that by the time he arrived in Delphi for the Pythian games, the officials thought he was dead. Source: *Greek Anthology* (Lucillius) 11.81.

Androsthenes. Greek pankratiast, 5th century, Maenalus. Androsthenes won two Olympic pankration championships; the first of these occurred in 420, and the second, presumably, in 416. SOURCES: Pausanias 6.6.1; Thucydides 5.49. (Thucydides goes on to give a detailed account of the breaking of the Olympic truce by the Spartans in 420, and the subsequent controversy surrounding that act. *See* Lichas.)

Anephedros. *See* Ephedros.

Anniceris. Greek charioteer, 4th century, Cyrene. Anniceris was such a skilled charioteer that he could circle Plato's Academy many times in his chariot, each time keeping the wheels in the same track as before. Plato and his friends were duly impressed. SOURCES: Aelian *Various Histories* 2.27; (Ps) Lucian *In Praise of Demosthenes* 23.

Antenor. Greek pankratiast. *See* Leontiscus.

Antias. Greek wrestler (?). *See* Thaeaus.

Antiloce. Roman charioteer. *See* Cresces.

Antipater. Greek boxer (boys'), [4th century], Miletus. After Antipater's Olympic boxing victory, the Syracusans attempted to bribe his father into proclaiming that Antipater hailed from Syracuse. But Antipater refused to cooperate in the scheme, instead inscribing on his victory statue his true origin, and adding that he was the first Ionian accorded the privilege of placing such a statue at Olympia. SOURCE: Pausanias 6.2.6.

Anystis. Greek long distance runner. *See* Phidippides.

Apis. Greek boxer, dates and place of origin unknown. Apis was so inept at boxing that his grateful rivals set up a statue in his honor. SOURCE: *Greek Anthology* (Lucillius) 11.80.

Apollonius. Greek boxer. *See* Heraclides.

Apollonius. Roman gladiator (Thracian), dates and place of origin unknown. One of the few left-handed gladiators. This characteristic was apparently sufficiently unusual and advantageous that it merited special mention on Apollonius' tombstone. *See* Lycus. SOURCE: *CIL* 6.10196.

Apollophanes. Greek boxer, dates and place of origin unknown. The rigors of boxing were well illustrated by the features of Apollophanes: a head like a sieve or a worm-eaten book, full of holes and scars, crooked and straight. SOURCE: *Greek Anthology* (Lucillius) 11.78.

Appuleius Diocles. Roman charioteer, born A.D.104, flourished 122–146, Lusitania. Diocles was certainly one of the most successful drivers in the history of Roman chariot racing. He is also one of the most well attested, the details of his career having been preserved in the form of a lengthy inscription. Diocles was 42 years, seven months and 23 days old when the inscription was made. Presumably, it served as a dedicatory plaque to commemorate his retirement from charioteering. Some have wrongly interpreted the inscription as a funerary monument, with the numbers referring to Diocles' age at death. However, both the format and the content militate against this view.

Diocles immigrated to Rome (apparently as a young man) where he began racing chariots in 122 as a member of the White faction. His first victory came two years later, while a member of the same faction. In 128, after 91 victories with the Whites in six years, he transferred to one of the most powerful factions, the Greens. But save for two minor victories in *bigae*, Diocles never won a race as a Green faction driver. At first glance, this is quite remarkable. It seems odd that a young and clearly promising charioteer would fail to triumph even once with one of the factions for which winning was habitual. Some possibilities:

1. The large numbers of skilled, veteran drivers surely employed by the Green faction rendered it difficult for a new man to establish himself, no matter how successful he might have been earlier in his career with the Whites.

2. Diocles in some way offended the owners or managers of the faction, and was therefore denied access to the best horses and equipment.

3. He was injured during his tenure with the Greens. After all, charioteering carried with it a great risk of bodily harm, and

physical disability would obviously hinder active participation on the racetrack.

In any case, the years 128 to 131 are the most poorly attested of his 24-year career. He spent some of that time with the Greens — but how much is uncertain — and he also served a brief stint with the Blues (for whom he won ten times) before moving on to the Reds, presumably in 130 or 131. It was with this faction that he spent the remainder of his career, until his retirement in 146.

Given these data, a few other assumptions may be made. If he retired as a charioteer at age 42, and raced chariots for 24 years, then: (1) he began his career at age 18; (2) he was born in 104; (3) he won his first race at age 20; (4) he switched from the Whites to the Greens at age 24; (5) he started winning regularly with the Reds at about age 27. (But *see* Special Essay 7, "How Long Was Diocles' Career?" on pages 119–120.)

Over the course of his 24 years as a driver, he engaged in 4,257 races, winning an astounding 1,462. His victory total certainly ranked him with Rome's best charioteers; indeed, the 1,000-victory plateau represented a major milestone, since a driver who had won that frequently was dubbed an *agitator miliarius*, a 1,000-race winner. Furthermore, in winning more than one-third of his starts, he outperformed the average driver by a considerable margin. The Circus Maximus, for example, could accommodate twelve chariots, which obviously meant that each driver had roughly one chance in twelve of winning.

The great majority of Diocles' triumphs were achieved in singles races, contests in which each driver competed for himself. Diocles' statistics suggest that singles races were the most common, and probably the most popular among individual charioteers.

Of Diocles' 1,064 singles victories, he won major cash awards 92 times:

Size of Award	Number of times won
30,000 sesterces	32
40,000 sesterces	28
50,000 sesterces	29
60,000 sesterces	3
	92

He also won 347 doubles races, and 51 triples races. The itemization of his win total according to singles, doubles and triples victories may be summarized thus: singles, 1,064; doubles, 347; triples, 51; total, 1,462.

In addition to his 1,462 victories, he placed second 861 times, third 576 times and fourth (for a 1,000 sesterces purse) once; he failed to place 1,351 times. The enumeration: firsts, 1,462; seconds, 861; thirds, 576; fail, 1,351; total, 4,250.

This is the only place in the first eleven lines of the inscription where a statistical inconsistency occurs. Seven contests are unaccounted for; according to line six, Diocles competed in 4,257 races. Previous commentators have demurred when faced with resolving this inconsistency. It might be explained thus:

Firsts:	1,462
Seconds:	861
Thirds:	576
Prize-winning fourths:	1
Victories in *bigae* (for the Reds):	3
Victories in *bigae* (for the Whites):	1
Victories in *bigae* (for the Greens):	2
Fail:	1,351
Total:	4,257

He utilized all the popular racing strategies, but he favored *occupavit et vicit*, with which he triumphed in 815 races. He also won 502 times employing the *eripuit et vicit* technique. And it is in this section of the inscription that the best indication appears that *eripuit et vicit* refers to a race in which two rival chariots raced neck-and-neck on the final lap, until one of them pulled ahead and snatched victory from the other. All 502 of Diocles' *eripuit* victories were earned at the expense of one of the other three factions: from the Greens, 216; from the Blues, 205; from the Whites, 81.

He won over 35,000,000 sesterces during his career, including three races offering a top prize of 60,000; 29 races with a 50,000 sesterce purse; and 28 races with a 40,000 sesterce purse.

He was also credited with a number of innovations and records. He won two races with six-horse teams (the standard number was four), and he triumphed with a seven-horse team, the first time such a yoking arrangement was ever employed. Not only did he use the seven-horse team, but he won a 50,000 sesterce prize with it.

He also surpassed the victory and prize money records set by other well-known drivers of his own and previous times. For example, a Green faction charioteer (whose name is lost due to a gap in the inscription) won 1,025 races, and additionally claimed the distinction of having been the first man up to that point to have won seven 50,000 sesterce prizes. Diocles shattered that record with his 29 victories in 50,000 sesterce races.

Also noted are the win totals of three of Diocles' rivals: Flavius Scorpus (q.v.), 2,048; Pompeius Musclosus, 3,559; and an unnamed driver who won 1,025. (The latter was very likely the same Green charioteer alluded to above.) Their cumulative victory total was 6,632, 28 of which brought them a prize of 50,000 sesterces. Although Diocles' number of career wins (1,462) was comparatively paltry, he took pride in the fact that his 29 victories in 50,000 sesterce races exceeded their combined total of 28 such wins.

A certain Pontius Epaphroditus won 1,467 times (five more than Diocles), but Diocles surpassed him in singles victories, 1,069 to 911. Diocles also gained more triumphs with the crowd-pleasing *eripuit et vicit* strategy, 502 to 467.

An inscription found at Praeneste suggests that Diocles may have lived there after his retirement as an active charioteer. Presumably the fortune that he earned would have enabled him to pursue any lifestyle he wished.

Diocles' claim to the grandiloquent title *omnium agitatorum eminentissimus* ("the most outstanding of all charioteers") seems justified by the available evidence.

Sources: *CIL* 6.10048; 14.2884. *See also* the comments of Friedlaender *Roman Life and Manners* (Vol. IV), pages 154–164, and Harris *Sport in Greece and Rome, page 198ff*.

Aratus. Greek chariot racer/pentathlete, 3rd century, Sicyon. As a young man, Aratus specialized in the pentathlon, winning numerous championships — Plutarch does not state when, where or how many — before turning his attention to the chariot race, where he was credited with an Olympic victory. His extensive military career is detailed in Plutarch's biography, and to a lesser degree, by Pausanias (2.8). Sources: Pausanias 6.12.5,6; Plutarch *Life of Aratus* 3.

Arcesilas. Greek chariot racer, 5th century, Cyrene. Arcesilas' driver Carrhotus (q.v.) overcame forty rival charioteers to win a victory at the Pythian games. His son, Lichas (q.v.), was also involved in chariot racing. Source: Pindar *Pythian* 5.

Archippus. Greek boxer, [late 4th or early 3rd century], Mitylene. Archippus had won men's boxing championships at all four crown festivals before reaching the age of 21. SOURCE: Pausanias 6.15.1.

Arena. (Literal meaning: "sand.") The central area of a Roman amphitheater, where the gladiatorial matches were fought; called the arena because it was surfaced with sand.

Aretippus. *See* Leucinas.

Aristeas. Greek wrestler/pankratiast. *See* Straton.

Aristeus. Greek dolichos racer. *See* Chimon.

Aristides. Greek diaulos/hoplite racer; dolichos racer — boys', dates unknown, Elis. Aristides won an Olympic championship in the armored race and a diaulos crown at the Pythian games. At Nemea, he triumphed in a race held in the hippodrome, a distance twice that of the diaulos. SOURCE: Pausanias 6.16.4.

Aristodemus. Greek wrestler, early 4th century, Elis. Aristodemus won the wrestling championship by default at the 98th Olympiad (388) when no challenger opposed him. SOURCES: Eusebius 205; Pausanias 6.3.4.

Aristomenes. Greek wrestler (boys'), mid-5th century, Aegina. Aristomenes won Olympic and Pythian wrestling championships, as well as victories in festivals at Marathon and Megara. His uncle Theognotus was an Olympic wrestling winner, while another uncle, Clitomachus, won an Isthmian crown in wrestling. SOURCE: Pindar *Pythian* 8.

Aristomenes. Greek wrestler/pankratiast. *See* Straton.

Aristonicus. Greek boxer. *See* Clitomachus.

Armored race. A kind of Greek foot race in which the runners wore helmets and carried shields.

Arrachion. *See* Arrhichion.

Arrhichion. (Sometimes spelled Arrachion). Greek pankratiast, mid-6th century, Phigalia. Arrhichion won pankration championships at the 56th and 55th Olympiads (572, 568), but his third consecutive Olympic crown (564) was the most memorable. In the final match of the day, Arrhichion's (unnamed) opponent managed to wrap his legs around Arrhichion's waist while simultaneously strangling him with his hands. Despite his rapidly weakening condition, Arrhichion was able to dislodge his opponent's grip long enough to dislocate his ankle — some sources say toe — with such force that his rival yielded. However, the strangling grip ultimately proved fatal, and Arrhichion expired. According to Philostratus, Arrhichion was on the point of conceding defeat when his trainer called out to him that it would be a noble posthumous honor to have never yielded at the Olympic games. Whether this bit of advice inspired Arrhichion to continue the match to the death is not stated; but he was indeed awarded the crown of victory posthumously. Sources: Eusebius 201; Pausanias 8.40.1–2; Philostratus *(On Gymnastics)* 21; Philostratus *(Images)* 2.6. There is some controversy and contradiction in the works of both ancient and modern writers concerning the exact circumstances and cause of Arrhichion's death. Those readers who might wish more detail on the matter should consult the ancient sources here listed, and R. Brophy's article "Deaths in the Pan-Hellenic Games: Arrachion and Creugas," in the *American Journal of Philology* 99 (1978), pages 363–390.

Artemidorus. Greek pankratiast, 1st century A.D., Tralles. Artemidorus failed in his first attempt to achieve Olympic success when he was defeated in the boys' pankration. But shortly after, at a festival in Smyrna, he had so increased his skill and strength that he won pankration championships in three divisions: boys', young men's, and men's. Artemidorus later atoned for his Olympic defeat as well, by winning the men's pankration at the 212th Olympiad (A.D. 68). Source: Pausanias 6.14.2–3.

Ascondas. Greek pankratiast. *See* Ephudion.

Astyanax. Greek pankratiast, 4th century, Miletus. Astyanax, winner of pankration crowns at three successive Olympiads, was once invited to dinner by the Persian Ariobarzanes. He vowed to consume all the food prepared for the eight other guests, and he subsequently made good on his vow. When the Persian asked him to perform some feat of strength, he broke off a bronze ornament from one of the couches, and flattened it barehanded. When he died, two funeral urns were required to contain his ashes. SOURCE: Athenaeus 4.135D; 10.413B. Eratosthenes states that Astyanax was six times *periodonikes* in the pankration, each time *akoniti*. Astyanax's name also appears in Menander's fragmentary play *Kolax*, where a scholiast's comment refers to him as the best pankratiast of his time.

Astylus. Greek stade/diaulos racer, early 5th century, Croton. Astylus won the stade and diaulos races in the Olympic games of 488, and successfully defended his championships in 484 and 480. However, in the latter two Olympiads, he represented Syracuse, apparently bribed to do so by the Syracusan king. For this misdeed, the citizens of Croton converted his house into a prison and removed his commemorative statue.

Like many other famous athletes, he avoided sexual relations while training for the Olympics.

SOURCES: Dionysius of Halicarnassus 8.1.; 8.77; Eusebius 203; Pausanias 6.13.1; Plato *Laws* 8.840A. (In 8.1, Dionysius calls him Astylus of Croton; in 8.77, after his change of fealty, Dionysius refers to him as Astylus of Syracuse.)

Attalus. Greek chariot racer, 3rd century, Pergamum. Attalus' Olympic victory is commemorated in an inscription, which is perhaps more noteworthy for its description of the starting system employed at Olympia: the chariots started from behind a rope barrier, removed to the accompaniment of a loud noise to signal the start of the race. SOURCE: *IAG* 37.

Aulus. Greek boxer, dates and place of origin unknown. The epigram on Aulus, although humorous, illustrates the brutality of boxing. Aulus dedicated his cracked skull to Zeus at Olympia, and would, if he survived, dedicate whatever vertebrae remained to him. *Greek Anthology* (Lucillius) 9.258.

Marcus Aurelius Asclepiades. Roman pankratiast, late 2nd century A.D., place of origin uncertain. Apparently, he came from Roman Egypt, although he claims or infers citizenship in Naples, Athens, Elis and several other places. He clearly specialized in Greek contests, but his Roman name suggests that he should be considered a Roman (not Greek) athlete.

Asclepiades asserts that he was *periodonikes*, and undefeated, in the pankration. He boasts that he never cheated, never complained, never triumphed *akoniti;* and that he won the pankration at the 240th Olympiad (A.D. 181), as well as once at the Pythian games, and twice each at the Isthmian and Nemean. He also states that he gained pankration championships at many other places, including Argos, Rome, Naples, Athens, Smyrna, Pergamum, Rhodes and Sparta. He retired at the age of 25, but later staged a comeback in which he won an additional pankration championship, in Alexandria. SOURCE: *IG* 14.1102. *See also* Harris' translation and commentary in *Greek Athletes and Athletics*, pages 127–129.

Aurelius Heraclides. Roman charioteer, no earlier than the 1st century B.C., place of origin unknown. Heraclides served as a driver for the Green faction, and later as a trainer for both the Green and Blue factions. (It seems likely that not a few charioteers were employed as trainers once their days as active charioteers had ended.) SOURCE: *CIL* 6.10057.

Marcus Aurelius Mollicius Tatianus. Roman charioteer, dates unknown, Rome. Tatianus died before his 21st birthday, but still compiled some remarkable statistics: 125 victories, including 89 for the Reds, 24 for the Greens, five for the Blues and seven for the Whites. He won two 40,000 sesterces prizes; the faction which he represented when he accomplished this is unknown. SOURCE: *CIL* 6.10049.

Marcus Aurelius Polynices. Roman charioteer, dates unknown, Rome. Polynices, who lived to the age of 29, won 739 races in his career, including 655 for the Red faction, 55 for the Green, 12 for the Blue and 17 for the White. He took first place three times in races offering a top prize of 40,000 sesterces, and 26 times in 30,000 sesterce races. He triumphed eight times with an eight-horse rig, nine times with a 10-horse rig, and three times with a seven-horse. SOURCE: *CIL* 6.10049.

Auriga. *See* Agitator.

Avilius Teres. Roman charioteer, flourished prior to the mid–2nd century A.D., place of origin unknown. *CIL* 6.10054, a very fragmentary inscription, commemorates the exploits of the charioteer Avilius Teres, whose name also appears in the inscription on Appuleius Diocles (q.v.).

The content of the inscription touches upon the high points of Teres' career, including his (uncertain) number of *eripuit* victories, a total which surpassed the 51 gained by a rival whose name and statistics are missing. There is a reference to 1,155 Green faction wins (but not gained by Teres), and how he in some way rivaled that total by his accomplishments in his own faction (presumably the Red, which is given as his faction in the Diocles inscription). Teres may have been an *agitator miliarius* (as the *CIL* editors suggest). Two of his favored yoke horses were an unnamed African, and a russet horse named Callidromus.

The inscription concludes with the words *T CCXXX*, restored by the *CIL* editors to *[vici]T CCXXX*, "he won 230," followed by the name Claudius. SOURCE: *CIL* 6.10054.

Bassus. Roman gladiator *(murmillo)*, dates unknown, probably from Spain, where the inscription was discovered. Bassus, and a fellow *murmillo*, Satur, were placed in a common grave; their monument was erected by a certain Cornelia Severa, most likely the wife of one of them. Satur fought 13 times, but the text gives no indication of victories; Bassus won once, but no information appears concerning his total number of bouts. SOURCE: *AEspA* 33 (page 126.)

Bato. Roman gladiator, 3rd century A.D., place of origin unknown. The emperor Caracalla forced Bato to fight three bouts in one day, a highly irregular occurrence. When Bato was killed in the last one, the emperor arranged a magnificent funeral for him. SOURCE: Dio Cassius 78.6.

Belistiche. (Many variant spellings for the name are to be found in the sources.) Greek chariot racer, 3rd century, Macedonia (although Athenaeus indicates Argos). Belistiche won the four-colt chariot race in the 128th Olympiad (268) and in the following Olympiad, she took the two-colt race, the first time such an event was run at Olympia. Athenaeus (13.596E) calls her a high-born Argive courtesan and a woman of great beauty; Plutarch (*Moral Essays* [753E]) implies a lower origin, asserting that she was bought (perhaps as a slave) in the public market, but that later, as the mistress of an Egyptian king, she was worshipped as a goddess in

Alexandria. Neither writer, however, alludes to her equestrian accomplishments. SOURCES: *Papyrus Oxyrrhyncus* 20.2082; Pausanias 5.8.11.

Bestiarius. A Roman beast fighter; one who fought against wild animals in a *venatio*.

Bigae. A kind of Roman racing chariot pulled by two horses.

Blue; Blues; Blue faction. *See* Faction.

Boxing. A Greek event similar to modern boxing to the extent that each competitor attempted to injure or exhaust his opponent by striking him with the fists. Greek boxing differed from the modern version in that there were no rounds, rest periods, rings, weight classes, or point systems. A winner was declared when one boxer was no longer physically able to continue the fray. Boxers were paired by lot; a single elimination format was utilized.

Boys' events; Boys' division. *See* Men's division.

Caligula. *See* Special Essay 3, pages 106–107.

Callias. Greek pankratiast, 5th century, Athens. Callias won one Olympic championship, two Pythian, five Isthmian, four Nemean and an unspecified number of Panathenaic victories. Pausanias records that in the Olympics of 472 (in which Callias won his lone Olympic crown), the pankration matches continued until nightfall because the pentathlon and chariot races ran overtime. Consequently, the order of contests was changed; the equestrian events and the pentathlon were moved to the day following the pankration. SOURCES: *IAG* 15; Pausanias 5.9.3; 6.6.1.

Callippus. Greek pentathlete, 4th century, Athens. At the Olympic games of 332, Callippus bribed his rivals. He was fined for this offense, but he retained an Athenian lawyer (Hyperides) to help him evade the punishment. The Eleans refused to rescind the fine, but still Callippus resisted paying; Athens, in fact, began a boycott of the games. It took a pronouncement from the oracle of Apollo at Delphi to induce the Athenians to end their boycott and remit the money. SOURCE: Pausanias 5.21.5.

Calpenus Quintus. Roman gladiator, 1st century B.C., probably from Rome. Calpenus, an ex-senator, performed at a gladiatorial show sponsored by Julius Caesar; his opponent was Furius Leptinus, a man from a praetorian family. The incident is instructive in that it illustrates that not all gladiators were drawn from the ranks of slaves, criminals or economically disadvantaged free citizens. SOURCE: Suetonius *Life of Caesar* 39. (Compare the unfortunate Fadius, a soldier who was drafted into service as a gladiator, and won two matches. For this deed, he was not only denied the salary promised him, but was subsequently executed for complaining about the injustice. *See* Cicero *Letters to Friends* 10.32.)

Caprus. Greek wrestler/boxer/pankratiast, 4th century, Elis. Caprus was the first Olympic competitor to win championships in wrestling and the pankration at the same festival. He defeated Clitomachus (q.v.) in the pankration, while in wrestling, he bested the defending champion, Paeanius of Elis. He gained a similar, same-day double victory at the Pythian games, in wrestling and boxing. SOURCE: Pausanias 5.21.10; 6.15.4, 10.

Carceres. (Literal meaning: "jail cells.") The starting gates at the Roman Circus Maximus and elsewhere.

Carpophorus. Roman *bestiarius*, 1st century A.D., place of origin unknown. A noted *bestiarius*, Carpophorus was equally adept at dispatching boars, bears, lions and panthers. He once killed twenty wild animals in one *venatio*. His deeds and his strength were supposedly comparable to those of Hercules. SOURCE: Martial *Concerning Spectacles* 15, 23, 27.

Carrhotus. Greek chariot racer (driver, not owner), 5th century, Cyrene. The fifth *Pythian* Ode of Pindar celebrates the chariot race victory of Arcesilas (q.v.) of Cyrene. However, the poet devotes a good deal of space to a graphic description of the skill of Arcesilas' driver, Carrhotus. He notes Carrhotus' deftness in guiding the horses around twelve grueling laps without damaging the bridles or the harness, and how he brought the chariot through to victory intact, although the astonishing number of 40 others crashed. Pindar rightly observes that Carrhotus deserves monumental praise. SOURCE: Pindar *Pythian* 5.

Catianus. Roman charioteer, 1st century A.D., place of origin unknown. The epigrammatist Martial mentions Catianus in a brief and ambiguous poem: "The chariot of the blue faction is slapped repeatedly with the whip, and does not run. You're doing great, Catianus." The standard interpretation: Catianus was holding back, having been bribed to do so, and hence to lose the race. It is quite possible, however, that he was merely employing the *succedere* racing strategy, allowing the other chariots to pass him in the hope that a final surge on the last lap or two would bring him the victory. SOURCE: Martial 6.46.

Celadus. Roman gladiator (Thracian), 1st century A.D., place of origin unknown. Celadus' name appears in several Pompeian graffiti, including *CIL* 4.4345, where he is described as "the ornament of the girls," and 4.4342, where he claims the title "heartthrob of the girls."

Cerinthus. Roman gladiator *(murmillo)*, dates unknown, Greece. The *murmillo* Cerinthus was trained at a gladiatorial school in Capua. He had two bouts (with no mention of victory or defeat) and died at the age of 25. The fact that Cerinthus was a Greek indicates that traffic in gladiators extended almost literally from one end of the Roman world to the other: a Greek fighter, trained in Italy, died in Spain (where his epitaph was discovered). SOURCE: *AEspA* 33 (page 128).

Chaeron. Greek wrestler, mid–4th century, Pellana. Despite winning four wrestling crowns at the Olympic games and two at the Isthmian, Chaeron was held in contempt by his fellow citizens. He had a hand in overthrowing Pellana's constitution and allowing Alexander the Great to set him up as a tyrant. If that were not bad enough, he ruled the city with an iron hand, exiling its best citizens, giving to slaves the property of their masters, and forcing wellborn women to marry slaves. SOURCES: Athenaeus 11.509B; Pausanias 7.27.7.

Chariot racing (Greek). *See* Equestrian events.

Charmus. Greek dolichos racer, dates and place of origin unknown. Charmus had his problems in a dolichos race in Arcadia, finishing seventh in a field of six runners. It seems that Charmus had a friend who ran alongside him shouting encouragement, and, although fully dressed, crossed the finish line ahead of Charmus. Nicarchus adds that if Charmus had had five such friends, he would have finished twelfth. SOURCE: *Greek Anthology* (Nicarchus) 11.82.

Charmus. Greek horse racer, dates and place of origin unknown. Charmus won the horse race at the Isthmian games, and in the hope that he might also prevail at Olympia, he dedicated to Poseidon the following items, used in his Isthmian victory: the horse's muzzle and *odontophorus* (a necklace consisting of strings of teeth); the horse's wand and comb, and his whip. SOURCE: *Greek Anthology* (Philodemus or Argentarius) 6.246.

Chilon. Greek wrestler, 4th century, Patrae. Chilon won two wrestling crowns at the Olympic games, four at the Isthmian, one (or two? *see below*) at the Pythian and three at the Nemean. He died in battle, either at Chaeronea (338) or Lamia (323). An inscription erected in his honor at Olympia reads as follows: "In wrestling only I alone conquered twice the men at Olympia and at Pytho [i.e., the Pythian games], thrice at Nemea, and four times at the Isthmus near the sea; Chilon of Patrae, son of Chilon, whom the Achaean folk buried for my valour when I died in battle." (Loeb Classical Library translation.) If the "twice" is understood distributively to govern both Olympia and Delphi, then it is likely that Chilon was twice *periodonikes.* SOURCE: Pausanias 6.4.6-7; 7.6.5. In his commentary on Pausanias, J. G. Frazer makes the interesting observation that the word *monopales* ("wrestling only") indicates that Chilon specialized in wrestling, thus distinguishing him from wrestler/pankratiasts and pentathletes.

Chimon. Greek wrestler, 5th century, Argos. Chimon won an Olympic victory in wrestling, but at the subsequent Olympiad, Taurosthenes (q.v.) of Aegina claimed the wrestling championship. According to Pausanias, a phantom resembling Taurosthenes appeared in Aegina that very day to announce the victory.

Chimon's son Aristeus was a champion dolichos runner.
SOURCE: Pausanias 6.9.3.

Chionis. Greek stade/diaulos racer, mid–7th century, Sparta. Chionis won four Olympic stade championships, including three in succession (664, 660, 656), the first man to accomplish this feat. He also won three diaulos crowns. Additionally, he was supposed to have long-jumped 52 feet, but the figure is dubious. *See* Phayllus. Sources: Eusebius 197; Pausanias 3.14.3; 4.23.4,10; 6.13.2.

Cimon. Greek chariot racer, 6th century, Athens. Cimon was banished from Athens — Herodotus does not state the reason — by the tyrant Pisistratus. While an exile, he won charioteering crowns at two successive Olympiads. After the second triumph, he permitted the credit to be transferred to Pisistratus, whereupon the tyrant allowed him to return to Athens. He subsequently won a third Olympic championship. After his death, Cimon's prizewinning mares were buried next to him; the only other charioteer with a similar burial arrangement was Euagoras of Sparta. Sources: Herodotus 6.103; Plutarch *Life of Cato the Elder* 5.

Circus. The structure in which chariot races were held. A Roman circus differed from the Greek hippodrome (q.v.), in that it contained a central dividing wall around which the chariots raced in a counterclockwise fashion.

Circus Maximus. The great chariot racetrack in Rome. It was built in the valley between the Palatine and Aventine Hills. Over the centuries, it underwent several remodelings; by the time of Augustus, its seating capacity had been increased to an estimated 250,000.

Cleander. Greek pankratiast (boys' [?]), 5th century, Aegina. In addition to his Isthmian pankration championship, Cleander recorded wins in festivals at Megara and Epidaurus. His cousin Nicocles won an Isthmian crown in boxing. Source: Pindar *Isthmian* 8.

Cleombrotus. Greek boxer, dates and place of origin unknown. Cleombrotus retired from boxing to marry a wife whose blows were fiercer than any he had endured at the crown festivals. Source: *Greek Anthology* (Lucillius) 11.79.

Cleomedes. Greek boxer, early 5th century, Astypalaea. In the boxing finals of the 72nd Olympiad (492), Cleomedes killed his opponent, Iccus of Epidaurus. He was convicted by the judges of excessive brutality and deprived of his crown. A violent and short-tempered man, Cleomedes returned home and marched directly to the local schoolhouse, whereupon he vented his wrath on one of the pillars supporting the roof. The pillar shattered; about sixty children were killed or injured by the falling rubble. The aggrieved parents chased Cleomedes to a temple of Athena, where he enclosed himself in a large chest. His pursuers broke open the chest, but Cleomedes had disappeared without a trace. SOURCES: Pausanias 6.9.6–8; Plutarch *Life of Romulus* 28.

Cleosthenes. Greek chariot racer, late 6th century, Epidamnus. Cleosthenes' chariot took the crown at the 66th Olympiad (516); in honor of the event, he dedicated a statue of himself, his charioteer, and the four horses, Phoenix, Cnacias, Samus and Corax. Cleosthenes was the first horse breeder from mainland Greece to dedicate a statue at Olympia. SOURCE: Pausanias 6.10.6–8.

Cleoxenus. Greek boxer, mid–3rd century, Alexandria. Cleoxenus won the boxing crown at the 135th Olympiad (240), enabling him to claim the title *periodonikes*. He completed the circuit without sustaining any injuries. SOURCE: Eusebius 207.

Clisthenes. Greek chariot racer, 6th century, Sicyon. Clisthenes used the renown he gained by winning the chariot race at Olympia in a unique manner, by publicly proclaiming that he would marry off his daughter Agarista to the best suitor in all of Greece. This offer attracted a number of interested young men from many locales — Herodotus lists all the names — but eventually, Clisthenes settled upon Megacles of Athens.

Clisthenes also won the chariot race at the Pythian games in the first Pythiad in which the event was held. SOURCES: Herodotus 6.126–131; Pausanias 10.7.7.

Clitomachus. Greek wrestler (5th century). *See* Aristomenes.

Clitomachus. Greek wrestler/boxer/pankratiast, 3rd century, Thebes. Clitomachus was credited with a number of noteworthy feats. At the Isthmian games, he won wrestling, boxing and pankration championships on the same day, a rare and exceedingly difficult accomplishment, unprecedented according to Alcaeus. He took the boxing and pankration crowns at the 141st Olympiad (216). In the Olympic games of 212, Clitomachus again entered both the boxing and pankration competitions, while one of his chief rivals, Caprus (q.v.) of Elis, declared for the wrestling and the pankration contests. After Caprus won the wrestling crown, Clitomachus appealed to the judges to reverse the order of events, and run the pankration before the boxing matches, thus enabling him to compete against Caprus without first having to endure the wounds and blows certain to come his way in boxing. The judges assented, but the result for Clitomachus was a disappointment, as he still lost to Caprus.

On another occasion, he faced an inferior Egyptian opponent, Aristonicus, in a match at Olympia. The Greek spectators cheered and supported the underdog, much to the chagrin of their country-man Clitomachus. The bout proceeded, with the two adversaries appearing to be evenly matched. Each time Aristonicus landed a blow, the crowd responded enthusiastically. Finally, Clitomachus yelled with some asperity to the onlookers that he was fighting for the glory of Greece, whereas Aristonicus represented an Egyptian king. He inquired of them whether they truly wished to see a foreigner win at Olympia. His speech had the desired effect; with the crowd on his side, Clitomachus defeated his opponent.

In his personal life, he maintained an attitude of self-discipline and moral rectitude, even to the extent that he customarily excused himself from social gatherings if the other guests began telling off-color jokes and stories.

SOURCES: Aelian *On Animals* 6.1; *Various Histories* 3.30; *Greek Anthology* (Alcaeus) 9.588; Pausanias 6.15.3–5; Plutarch *Moral Essays* 710D; Polybius 27.9.

Clitostratus. Greek wrestler, 2nd century, Rhodes. Clitostratus' method of winning in wrestling was to apply a stranglehold to his opponent, and then suddenly throw him. SOURCE: Eusebius 209.

Coliseum. *See* Flavian Amphitheater.

Columbus. Roman gladiator *(murmillo)*, 1st century A.D., place of origin unknown. Columbus ("The Dove") won a gladia-torial bout in which he suffered a slight injury. But the emperor Caligula, who disliked *murmillones*, ordered poison to be smeared into the wound, thus accomplishing what Columbus' opponent could not. SOURCE: Suetonius *Life of Caligula* 55.

Comaeus. Greek boxer, mid–7th century, Megara. Comaeus won the boxing championship at the 32nd Olympiad (652) by defeating three brothers in succession. (The brothers' names are not preserved.) SOURCE: Eusebius 197.

Commodus. *See* Special Essay 3, pages 107–108.

Contrarete. (Literal meaning: "against a *retiarius*.") As the literal meaning implies, a *contrarete* was a kind of Roman gladiator — probably heavily armed — matched against a *retiarius*.

Corax. Roman charioteer, mid–1st century A.D., place of origin unknown. At the Secular Games of A.D. 47, Corax ("The Raven"), a charioteer for the White faction, was thrown from his chariot at the start of the race. His horses, however, stayed the course despite the absence of human control, and finished the race in proper fashion. SOURCE: Pliny the Elder 8.160. (In the following sections, Pliny relates two other stories about the feats of driverless teams. In one of these, a charioteer named Ratumenna had been thrown at a race in Veii; the horses ran from there to Rome and galloped around the Capitoline Hill.)

Coroebus. Greek stade racer, 8th century, Elis. Coroebus, a cook by trade, was the winner of the stade at what is generally thought to have been the first Olympiad in 776. (The stade was the only Olympic event until the celebration of the 14th Olympiad in 724.) His prize was an apple, not an olive wreath, wreath prizes not being awarded until the sixth Olympiad. On Coroebus' tomb, there was an inscription stating that he was the first man to win an Olympic victory, and that the site of his grave marked the limit of Elean territory. SOURCES: Athenaeus 9.382B; Eusebius 193; Pausanias 5.8.6; 8.26.3–4; Phlegon *FGH* 257.1.

Crauxidas. Greek horse racer, 7th century, Crannon. Horse racing was established as an Olympic event at the 33rd Olympiad (648), and Crauxidas won it. SOURCE: Pausanias 5.8.8.

Cres. *See* Four brother athletes.

Crescens. Roman charioteer, born A.D. 102, flourished 115–124, Maurus. Crescens, a Blue faction charioteer, won his first victory in 115, on the 8th of November; he drove a quadriga pulled by Circius, Acceptor, Delicatus and Cotynus. By 124 (apparently the year in which he died), he had participated in 686 races, winning 47, including 19 singles victories, 23 doubles and five triples. He employed the *occupavit* technique eight times for wins, *eripuit* 38 times, and *praemisit* once.

In addition to his 47 wins, he placed second 30 times and third on 111 occasions. He earned a total of 1,558,346 sesterces.

He died at the age of 22, after nine years as a charioteer, thus indicating that he began his career at 13.

Source: *CIL* 6.10050.

Crescens. Roman gladiator *(retiarius)*, 1st century A.D., place of origin unknown. Crescens is mentioned in several Pompeian graffiti. In one, he is called the *puparrum dominus,* "master of fair young women," and in another, the *puparrum nocturnarum...*, "master of the nightly...." Unfortunately, the remainder is not extant. Sources: *CIL* 4.4353; 4356.

Cresces. Roman charioteer, dates unknown, place of origin unknown (possibly Britain, where the inscription was found). The name Cresces, followed by the letters *Av* (*ave*, "hail"), appears with the names of three other charioteers, Hierax, Olympae and Antiloce; their names are all designated with *Va* (*vale*, "farewell"). Apparently, the latter three were charioteers whom Cresces had defeated. Source: *CIL* 7.1273. *See also* Martial 3.95, for a similar usage of *ave*.

Crethus. *See* Four brother athletes.

Creugas. Greek boxer. *See* Damoxenus.

Crison (sometimes spelled Crisson). Greek stade racer, 5th century, Himera. Crison dominated the stade at Olympia in the sixth decade of the fifth century, winning it in 448, 444 and 440. He was well known to Socrates, who noted that if he were to race against Crison, it would be interesting only if Crison held back. Socrates' comment: "I can't run fast, but he can run slow." And he did precisely that, in a foot race against a certain Alexander, who was insulted that Crison had deliberately slowed the pace.

Like a number of noted Greek athletes, Crison abstained from sexual activity while training.

Sources: Diodorus Siculus 12.5; 12.23; 12.29 (where he wrongly asserts that Crison won for the second time, instead of the third);

Dionysius of Halicarnassus 11.1; Eusebius 203; Pausanias 5.23.4;
Plutarch *Moral Essays* 58F; 471F; Plato *Laws* 840A; *Protagoras*
335E–336A.

Crisson. *See* Crison.

Crown festivals. Each year, hundreds of communities in the
Greek world sponsored organized athletic competitions, often offer-
ing to the victors monetary prizes or other forms of compensation.
However, the four most prestigious festivals — the Olympic,
Pythian, Nemean and Isthmian games — rewarded champions with
leaf crowns. Hence, the designation crown festival.

Cylon. Greek diaulos racer, 7th century, Athens. Cylon won
an Olympic championship in the diaulos, and later used his prominence as an athlete as a pretext for meddling in Athenian politics.
A typically ambiguous oracular pronouncement from Delphi had
stated that he and his adherents were to take over the Athenian
Acropolis during a "great festival of Zeus." Cylon interpreted this to
refer to the next Olympiad, given that the Olympic games were
dedicated to Zeus; the fact that he was an Olympic champion
seemed to afford additional credibility to the pronouncement. He
never considered the possibility that the "great festival of Zeus"
might not have been a reference to the Olympic games and their con-
comitant religious observances.
    In any case, he attempted to carry out his plan at the subse-
quent Olympiad; it failed miserably. Cylon and his supporters were
blockaded on the Acropolis. Although Cylon himself escaped,
his less fortunate followers were treacherously murdered by the be-
siegers, under the leadership of Megacles. (Thus began a long and
famous family feud between the descendants of Megacles and
Cylon.)
    SOURCES: Eusebius 197; Herodotus 5.71; Pausanias 1.28.1; Plu-
tarch *Life of Solon* 12; Thucydides 1.126.

Cynisca. Greek chariot racer, early 4th century, Sparta.
Cynisca, sister of the Spartan king Agesilaus, was extremely desir-
ous of winning victories at Olympia. She became the first woman
to breed horses, and the first to win a crown of victory at Olympia
in chariot racing (presumably as owner, not driver); according to
Xenophon, she was the only woman in Greece ever to taste Olympic

success in that event. Pausanias asserts that other women gained Olympic triumphs, but none ever equalled Cynisca's skill or fame. Plutarch, however, says that Agesilaus persuaded her to compete at Olympia to illustrate that attaining victory there did not stem from one's ability, but came simply as a result of having money and the willingness to spend it. SOURCES: *Greek Anthology* (Anonymous) 13.16; *IAG* 17; Pausanias 3.8.1–2; 3.15.1; 5.12.5; 6.1.6; Plutarch *Life of Agesilaus* 20; Xenophon *Agesilaus* 9.6.

Damagetus. Greek pankratiast. *See* Diagoras.

Damaretus. Greek Hoplite racer, late 6th century, Heraea. Damaretus captured crowns in the armored races of the 65th and 66th Olympiads (520, 516). He was the first athlete to win this event; its inaugural year was 520. His statue portrayed him decked out in a helmet and shin guards, and carrying a shield; in later times, armored racers did not wear headgear or greaves.

Damaretus' son Theopompus was a successful pentathlete, and his grandson, also named Theopompus, was a champion wrestler. SOURCES: Eusebius 201; Pausanias 5.8.10; 6.10.4–5; 8.26.2; 10.7.7; Philostratus 13.

Damatrius. Greek stade/dolichos racer, [3rd century], Tegea. Among his many footracing victories, Damatrius was credited with one stade and one dolichos win at Olympia. He also triumphed four times at Nemea, twice at the Isthmian games and twice at the Pythian. SOURCE: *IAG* 44.

Damiscus. Greek foot racer (boys')/pentathlete, dates unknown, Messenia. Damiscus was a mere 12 years of age when he won his Olympic victory. He was only the third Messenian to triumph at Olympia, the others being Leontiscus (q.v.) and Symmachus. Later, as a pentathlete, he triumphed at the Nemean and Isthmian games. SOURCE: Pausanias 6.2.10–11.

Damonon. Greek stade/diaulos/dolichos racer; chariot racer, 5th century, Sparta. In a highly self-congratulatory inscription, Damonon records a number of foot racing and equestrian victories, all gained at festivals of little or no competitive significance. His son, Enymachratidas, was equally successful, as a participant in all three kinds of foot races. SOURCE: *IAG* 16.

Damoxenus. Greek boxer, dates unknown, Syracuse. A match at the Nemean games featuring Damoxenus and Creugas of Epidamnus dragged on until nightfall. In order to finish their bout before darkness enveloped them, each boxer agreed to allow the other to strike one unobstructed blow. Creugas went first, punching Damoxenus in the head. Damoxenus then ordered Creugas to raise his arm; the latter complied. Damoxenus then jabbed Creugas in the ribs, his sharpened fingernails enabling him to pierce Creugas' innards. He disemboweled his unfortunate rival, who forthwith expired. Damoxenus was disqualified for this act of barbarism, and the crown was awarded posthumously to Creugas. SOURCE: Pausanias 8.40.3–5. (In 8.40.3, Pausanias provides a clear description of the hand coverings — *himantes* — worn by Greek boxers; thin strips of braided ox-hide wrapped around the palm of the hand and the knuckles, leaving the fingers exposed.) *See also* the source references on Arrhichion for additional bibliographical information.

Dandes. Greek stade racer, 5th century, Argos. Dandes was a highly successful stade racer, counting among his triumphs two at the Olympic games, three at the Pythian, two at the Isthmian and 15 at the Nemean, as well as numerous wins at other festivals. SOURCES: Diodorus Siculus 11.53; Dionysius of Halicarnassus 9.37; *Greek Anthology* (Simonides) 13.14. (Moretti observes that some of Dandes' fifteen Nemean triumphs would likely have been gained at the same festivals, but in several running events.)

Demostratus. Greek wrestler, dates unknown, Sinope. Demostratus won two championships at the Isthmian games. In the course of his wrestling career, he was never thrown. SOURCE: *Greek Anthology* (Philippus) 16.25.

Diagoras. Greek boxer, 5th century, Rhodes. Diagoras, patriarch of a famous family of athletes, won a boxing championship at the Olympic games of 464. He also gained championships at the Isthmian games (four in all), and at Aegina, Arcadia, Argos, Athens, Pellana and Thebes.

His three sons were also noted heavy eventers: Acusilaus, in boxing; Damagetus, in the pankration; Dorieus (q.v.), also in the pankration. Dorieus won crowns at three consecutive Olympiads (432–424), as well as eight Isthmian and seven Pythian victories. Diagoras' grandsons Eucles (396) and Pisirodus (388) also won Olympic boxing championships. It is said that Acusilaus and Damagetus, having triumphed at the same Olympiad, hoisted their father onto their shoulders and carried him through the crowd, who tossed flowers at him and congratulated him on his sons' excellence. Cicero and Plutarch both relate the following incident from Diagoras' old age: On the day when he had seen his two sons crowned at Olympia, a Spartan supposedly approached him and said, "Die, Diagoras, for you could never ascend to heaven." The point seemed to be that Diagoras had reached the apex of happiness, and nothing – not even heaven itself – could surpass the joy a father would feel at the Olympic success of his offspring. Sources: Cicero *Tusculan Disputations* 1.46; Pausanias 6.7.1–4; Plutarch *Life of Pelopidas* 34; Pindar *Olympian 7*.

Diallus. Greek pankratiast (boys'), dates unknown, Smyrna. Diallus claimed to have been the first Ionian to win a crown in the boys' pankration. Source: Pausanias 6.13.6.

Diaulos. Sometimes called the double-pipe or double-stade, it was a Greek two-lap foot race covering approximately 400 yards.

Dicon. Greek stade racer, early 4th century, Caulonia. Dicon won 15 crown festival championships: five at the Pythian games, three at the Isthmian, four at the Nemean and three at the Olympic. Although a native of Caulonia, he was bribed to declare himself a Syracusan, and he represented Syracuse at the crown festivals. (There is no record of any punishment given him for this act. Compare the harsh treatment accorded men like Astylus [q.v.] and Lichas [q.v.] for attempting similar changes of citizenship.) Sources: Diodorus Siculus 15.14; Eusebius 205; *Greek Anthology* (Anonymous) 13.15, where he is credited with only two Olympic victories; Pausanias 6.3.11.

Diocles. *See* Four brother athletes.

Diocles of Messenia. Greek stade racer, 8th century, Messenia. Diocles, winner of the stade in the 7th Olympiad (752), was the first Olympic champion to receive an olive crown prize. (Prior to this, apples were awarded to winners.) Sources: Dionysius of Halicarnassus 1.71; Eusebius 195.

Diognetus. Greek boxer, dates unknown, Crete. Diognetus killed his opponent, a certain Hercules, during a match. He was subsequently disqualified and expelled from Olympia, apparently for violating the rule against excessive violence. Despite his banishment, however, he was still held in high esteem by his fellow citizens. SOURCE: Photius 190 [65].

Dionysia. Greek stade racer, mid-1st century A.D., Tralles Caesarea. Dionysia, sister of Tryphosa (q.v.) and Hedea (q.v.), won a stade championship at the Isthmian games, and another one at Epidaurus. SOURCE: *IAG* 63.

Dionysidorus. Identified only as *Olympionikes*, Greek Olympian winner, 4th century, Thebes. Dionysidorus, acting as a Theban ambassador to Persia, was captured in Marathus by Alexander the Great. He was subsequently released, partly because of Alexander's compassion for Thebes, but also because of his respect for anyone who could gain an Olympic victory. SOURCE: Arrian 2.15.

Dioxippus. Greek pankratiast, 4th century, Athens. Dioxippus won an *akoniti* pankration victory in the Olympic games of 336. In his personal life, however, he did not fare as well.

His sister was accused of infidelity on the very day when she was supposed to be married. The man with whom she allegedly committed this act used as part of his defense the sheer folly of seducing the woman when her brother Dioxippus, and another heavy eventer, Euphraeus, were present; these two athletes were reputedly the strongest men in Greece.

Later, Dioxippus became a favorite of Alexander the Great, and accompanied him on his Persian campaigns. During a banquet, one of Alexander's Macedonian friends, Coragus by name, challenged Dioxippus to single combat. The other diners loudly applauded the idea, and so Dioxippus had little choice but to agree to the match.

On the appointed day, Coragus appeared on the field of battle decked out in his expensive armor, equipped with javelin, spear and sword; but Dioxippus, in true Olympic style, wore nothing but body oil, and carried no weapon save a club.

Coragus made the first move, hurling his javelin at Dioxippus, but the Athenian ducked as the missile flew harmlessly past him. Next, Coragus charged at Dioxippus with his spear, but Dioxippus shattered it with his club. Finally, Coragus reached for his sword, but before he could withdraw it from its scabbard, Dioxippus jumped on him, grabbed his swordhand, upended him and dropped him to the ground. He then placed his foot on the Macedonian's neck, raised his club in triumph, and awaited the reaction of the onlookers.

Alexander ordered Coragus to be set free, but he and the other Macedonians were clearly annoyed over the defeat of one of their own at the hands of an Athenian. In the days that followed, their hostility toward Dioxippus increased, until finally they devised a way to rid themselves of the famous pankratiast. They ordered a servant to plant a golden cup in Dioxippus' bed chamber, and when the cup was "discovered" the next evening during a banquet, they accused him of theft.

Dioxippus saw through the trick, but could not figure out how to exonerate himself. So after a short while he returned to his room, wrote a letter to Alexander describing the false accusation, and then committed suicide.

SOURCES: Aelian *Various Histories* 10.22; 12.58; Diodorus Siculus 17.100–101; Diogenes Laertius 6.43; *Papyrus Oxyrhynchus* 13.1607; Plutarch *Moral Essays* 521B.

Discus throw. One of the five events of the Greek pentathlon. Ancient discoboloi used much the same throwing techniques and equipment as their modern counterparts. Distance, not accuracy, was the desideratum.

Doctor. *See* Lanista.

Dolichos. A Greek long distance foot race. The distance varied from festival to festival. It may have been as short as three-quarters of a mile, to as long as three miles. However, ultra-long distance races (analogous to modern marathons, for example) were never run at ancient athletic meetings.

Dorieus. Greek pankratiast (and boxer?), 5th century, Rhodes. Dorieus, the youngest son of the boxer Diagoras (q.v.), won pankration championships at three consecutive Olympiads. He also earned eight Isthmian crowns, seven Nemean crowns, and an *akoniti* championship at the Pythian games, all presumably in the pankration. The evidence that some of these victories came in boxing rests on a very fragmentary inscription for an athlete whose name has been obliterated from the stone. Some scholars, however, insist that Dorieus was the man in question.

Dorieus fought on the Spartan side during the Peloponnesian War, an act which did little to enhance his popularity in Athens. However, when he was subsequently captured and brought to Athens, the Athenians were so awed by his presence that they released him unharmed.

Dorieus was later executed by the Spartans, who suspected him of treachery.

SOURCES: *Greek Anthology* 13.11 (attributed to Simonides, but this is unlikely, given that Simonides had already died when Dorieus was in his athletic prime); *IAG* 23; Pausanias 6.7.1, 4–7; Thucydides 3.8; 8.35; Xenophon *Hellenica* 1.1; 1.5.

Doubles race. A kind of Roman chariot race in which two drivers from the same faction cooperated with each other in an attempt to gain victory for one of them. *See also* singles race; triples race.

Dromeus. Greek dolichos racer, [5th century], Stymphalus. In addition to his athletic prowess — Dromeus won twice each at the Olympic and Pythian games, three times at the Isthmian and five times at the Nemean — he was a dietary innovator. Prior to his time, athletes ate primarily dairy products; Dromeus was the first to consume meat as part of his dietary regimen. SOURCE: Pausanias 6.7.10.

Dromeus. Greek pankratiast, 5th century, Mantinea. Dromeus' Olympic pankration victory in 480 was gained *akoniti*, the first time in Olympic history in which that had happened. (Pausanias records only one other *akoniti* pankration win in the crown festivals: Dorieus' [q.v.] Pythian triumph.) SOURCE: Pausanias 6.11.4.

Enymachratidas. Greek foot racer. *See* Damonon.

Epaphroditus. Roman charioteer, 1st century A.D., place of origin unknown. Epaphroditus' major faction was the Red, for whom he won 178 races. He also won eight times as a member of Domitian's short-lived Purple faction. SOURCE: *CIL* 6.10062.

Epharmostus. Greek wrestler, 5th century, Opus. Epharmostus won championships in wrestling at the Olympic, Isthmian and

Nemean games, and also distinguished himself at festivals at a number of other places, including Arcadia, Argos, Athens, Marathon and Pellana. SOURCE: Pindar *Olympian 9*. A scholiast's comment on Pindar indicates that Epharmostus also won once at Delphi (in 466).

Ephedros. (Literal meaning: "sitting beside.") The Greek sports wrestling, boxing and the pankration were conducted like single-elimination tournaments. If there were an odd number of contestants, the one man who received a bye was considered to have been *ephedros*, "sitting beside," while the other athletes competed. All competitors were matched by drawing lots; byes were assigned in the same manner. A particularly prestigious championship was one which was gained *anephedros*, "without sitting beside," i.e. one in which the athlete fought in every elimination round without ever drawing a bye.

Ephudion. Greek pankratiast, 5th century, Maenalus. Ephudion is mentioned several times by Aristophanes as an example of an old man who nonetheless was able to defeat a younger opponent, Ascondas. SOURCE: Aristophanes *Wasps* 1191–1194; 1383–1386.

Epitherses. Greek boxer, late 3rd or early 2nd century, Erythrae. Epitherses won two Olympic boxing championships, two more at the Pythian games, and one each at the Isthmian and Nemean games. SOURCES: *IAG* 46; Pausanias 6.15.6.

Eques. (Literal meaning: "horseman"; "knight.") A kind of Roman gladiator who fought on horseback; he was equipped with body armor, a shield, tunic, visored helmet and a spear.

Equestrian events. There was a wide array of Greek equestrian events; the number and kind varied from one festival to the next. The Olympic games originally featured a four-horse chariot race and a horse race. Three contests were added in the fifth century: a two-horse chariot race, a mule-drawn chariot race, and an event known as the *kalpe*, described by Pausanias as a horse race in which the riders dismounted at the end and finished the course by running alongside the horses. The latter two were eventually dropped from the Olympic program.

Other festivals offered competitions in two-horse and two-colt chariot races, four-colt chariot races, and ridden colt races.

Races were held in hippodromes, usually little more than large open spaces marked out with a turning post and a start/finish line. H. A. Harris (*Sport in Greece and Rome,* p. 162) suggests that 60 chariots could participate in one race at Olympia, while Pindar describes the crash of 40 chariots in a race at the Pythian games.

Unlike the track and field events, the driver of a chariot or the rider of a horse did not receive the crown if he won. Rather, the award went to the owner of the chariot or horse. (Unless otherwise noted, all the Greek individuals credited with equestrian victories were the owners, not the drivers or riders.)

Equus anagonus. The precise meaning of this Roman chariot racing term has not been established, but it probably refers to a horse which had never raced.

Equus centenarius. An honorary term for a Roman charioteering horse credited with 100 or more victories.

Equus ducenarius. An honorary term for a Roman charioteering horse credited with 200 or more victories.

Ergoteles. Greek dolichos racer, 5th century, Himera. Ergoteles won the dolichos at the 75th and 77th Olympiads (472, 464). He also numbered among his crown festival wins two at the Pythian games and one each at the Isthmian and Nemean games.

Ergoteles was originally from Cnossus in Crete. He was expelled from the island through the efforts of a rival political faction, eventually settling in Himera, where he became a model citizen. Hence, it was appropriate that Himera be listed as his hometown in the literary references to him.

SOURCES: Pausanias 6.4.11; Pindar *Olympian* 12.

Eripuit et vicit. (Literal meaning: "he tore away and won.") The exact application of this term to Roman chariot racing is uncertain, but it probably refers to a race in which two drivers were engaged in a tight struggle for the victory near the end of the race, until one of them managed to break away and win. (*See* Special Essay 7, pages 119–120, for additional discussion of this term.)

Essedarius. A kind of Roman gladiator who fought from a chariot. Two chariots were typically involved, with two men riding in each of the chariots: a driver and the gladiator. When the chariots drew near one another, the gladiators dismounted—either through compulsion or volition — to engage each other, while drivers and chariots waited nearby.

Euagoras. Greek two-horse chariot racer, late 5th century, Elis. Euagoras won the two-horse chariot race at the 93rd Olympiad (408), the first year in which the event was run. SOURCE: Xenophon *Hellenica* 1.2.

Euagoras (of Sparta). Greek chariot racer. *See* Cimon.

Eualces. Greek stade racer (boys'), early 4th century, Athens. Eualces was permitted to enter the boys' stade through the intercession of the Spartan king Agesilaus. Eualces' stature and strength suggested either that he was too old for the boys' event, or that he would easily dominate it — the sources are unclear on this point — but after much politicking, Agesilaus was able to gain eligibility for him. Oddly, neither Xenophon nor Plutarch mentions whether he won. SOURCES: Plutarch *Life of Agesilaus* 13; Xenophon *Hellenica* 4.1.

Euanoridas. Greek wrestler (boys'), dates unknown, Elis. Euanoridas, winner of the boys' wrestling at Olympia and Nemea, later became an umpire, and also a recorder of the names of Olympic champions. SOURCE: Pausanias 6.8.1.

Eubotas. Stade racer/Greek chariot racer, late 5th century, Cyrene. According to an oracular prophecy, Eubotas was to win an Olympic victory in the stade race. Based on that information, he commemorated his victory statue prior to the race. When he did indeed triumph (408), he was accorded the rare honor of winning a championship and dedicating his statue on the same day.

He is also said to have won a charioteering championship in the same Olympiad, but the presiding officials refused to recognize its legitimacy, claiming that the (evidently unqualified) Arcadians had administered the race.

SOURCES: Aelian *Various Histories* 10.2; Diodorus Siculus 13.68; Eusebius 203; Pausanias 6.8.3; Xenophon *Hellenica* 1.2.

Eucles. Greek long distance runner, 5th century, Athens. According to Plutarch, Eucles was the messenger who ran fully armed from Marathon to Athens to announce Athens' victory over the Persians at the Battle of Marathon (490). The only words he uttered before collapsing and dying were "*Chaerete, nicomen,*" "Hail! We've won!" SOURCE: Plutarch *Moral Essays* 347C. (This first "Marathon run" is often credited to Phidippides [q.v.], apparently on the basis of a fleeting reference in Lucian's short essay *A Slip of the Tongue in Greeting* 3, where the name is given as Philippides.)

Eucles. Greek boxer. *See* Diagoras.

Eudelus. Greek heavy eventer. *See* Straton.

Euphraeus. Greek pankratiast. *See* Dioxippus.

Eupolemus. Greek stade racer/pentathlete, early 4th century, Elis. Eupolemus' Olympic stade race victory in 396 was challenged by one of his opponents, Leon of Ambracia. The race was apparently very close, with two of the three judges on the scene voting to grant the win to Eupolemus. Leon appealed the decision to the Olympic Council, which subsequently fined the two judges who favored Eupolemus. (It should not be assumed that the Elean *Hellanodicae* were at all times impartial. Both Herodotus (2.160) and Diodorus Siculus (1.95) relate the story of a delegation of Eleans sent to Egypt to ask the king's advice on ways in which the fairness of the Olympic games could be assured. The response: prohibit Elean athletes from participating. The advice obviously was not taken.)

Eupolemus also won three championships in the pentathlon, two at the Pythian games, and another at the Nemean games. SOURCES: Diodorus Siculus 14.54, where the name is given as Eupolis; Eusebius 203; Pausanias 6.3.7; 8.45.4.

Eupolus. Greek boxer, 4th century, Thessaly. Eupolus had the dubious distinction (in 388) of being the first Olympic athlete to be convicted of bribing his rivals (Agenor of Arcadia, Prytanis of Cyzicus and Phormio of Halicarnassus, the boxing champion in the previous Olympiad). For this offense, all four boxers were fined; the money was used to fashion six bronze images of Zeus, placed near the stadium. SOURCE: Pausanias 5.21.2–3.

Euripus. *See* Spina.

Eurybatus. Greek wrestler, late 8th century, Sparta. Eurybatus won the wrestling crown in the 18th Olympiad (708), the first year in which wrestling competitions were held. SOURCES: Pausanias 5.8.7; Philostratus 12.

Eutelidas. Greek pentathlete/wrestler, 7th century, Sparta. Eutelidas, competing in the boys' division, won the pentathlon of the 38th Olympiad (628), the only year in which boys were permitted to enter that event. He also won a championship in boys' wrestling in the same festival. SOURCES: Eusebius 199, where the name is given as Deutelidas; Pausanias 5.9.1; 6.15.8; Plutarch *Moral Essays* 675C; Philostratus 13.

Euthymenes. Greek boxer or pankratiast. *See* Pytheas.

Euthymus. Greek boxer, early 5th century, Western Locri. Euthymus won boxing championships at the 74th, 76th and 77th Olympiads (484, 476, 472). In the games of 480, he lost — and it was the only defeat of his career — to Theagenes (q.v.), but the latter's victory was tainted: Theagenes had entered both the boxing and pankration contests that year, and was so exhausted from his match with Euthymus that he could not compete creditably in the pankration. The judges determined that he had signed on for the boxing merely to spite Euthymus; thereupon, they ordered him to pay Euthymus the sum of one talent as compensation.

Later in life, Euthymus fought a battle of a different sort. It was said that one of Odysseus' sailors, when visiting the southern Italian town of Temesa, became inebriated and raped one of the local women; for this offense he was stoned to death. But his ghost remained to plague the residents of the town until they agreed to present him with an annual gift: the most beautiful woman in town for his wife. Euthymus happened to visit Temesa at the very time when the townspeople were about to carry out the gruesome annual ceremony. Feeling pity for the unfortunate maiden to be offered that year, he resolved to fight the ghost for her. He did so successfully, and later married her.

According to Pliny, his statues at Olympia and his hometown of Locri were once struck by lightning on the same day, an unprecedented event. As a result, sacrifices were offered to him both while he was living and after his death. SOURCES: Aelian *Various Histories* 8.18; *IAG* 13; Pausanias 6.6.4–10; Pliny the Elder 7.152; Strabo 6.255.

Eutychus. Roman charioteer, 1st century A.D., place of origin unknown. As an example of the emperor Caligula's devotion to the

Green faction, he presented one of its drivers, this Eutychus, a gift of two million sesterces at a banquet. Source: Suetonius *Life of Caligula* 55.

Exaenetus. (Spelled Exagentus in Eusebius.) Greek stade racer, late 5th century, Acragas. Exaenetus won stade victories at the 91st and 92nd Olympiads (416, 412). Upon his return to Acragas after his triumph in 412, he was escorted into the city by a procession numbering 300 chariots, each one pulled by two white horses. Sources: Aelian *Various Histories* 2.8; Diodorus Siculus 12.82; 13.34; 13.82; Eusebius 203.

Exagentus. *See* Exaenetus.

Faction. Roman charioteers were grouped into four teams called factions, which supplied horses, chariots and all other equipment. Originally, there were but two factions, the Red and the White, but at some undetermined point in the first century B.C., two more factions emerged, the Blue and the Green. The emperor Domitian (reigned A.D. 81–96) expanded the league by adding the Purple and Gold factions, but these died out soon after the demise of their founder.

Fadius. Roman gladiator. *See* Calpenus Quintus.

Familia. (Literal meaning: "family"; "troupe.") A quasi-militaristic grouping into which Roman charioteers and especially gladiators were occasionally organized.

Felix. Roman charioteer, 1st century B.C., place of origin unknown. Pliny refers to the funeral of Felix, a Red faction charioteer, to illustrate the intense partisanship inspired by Roman chariot racing: A distraught backer of the Reds committed suicide by throwing himself on Felix' burning pyre. The opponents of the Reds, however, tried to discredit the story by claiming that the man had fainted and accidentally fell into the fire. Source: Pliny the Elder 7.186.

Flamma. Roman gladiator *(secutor)*, dates unknown, Syria. Flamma lived 30 years and engaged in 34 bouts, 21 of which resulted in victories, 13 in draws. Source: *CIL* 10.7297.

Flavian Amphitheater. The great Roman amphitheater (not called the Coliseum until the Middle Ages), its construction was initiated by the emperor Vespasian, and completed by his son, Titus. (Their family name was Flavius; hence Flavian.) The seating areas could be protected by retractable canopies in the event of inclement weather; the arena floor could be flooded for mock sea battles. The dedication of the amphitheater in A.D. 80 was celebrated by a costly gladiatorial show and a *venatio* which featured 5,000 wild beasts.

Flavius Scorpus. Roman charioteer, 1st century A.D., place of origin unknown. According to the inscription pertaining to Appuleius Diocles (q.v.), Scorpus won 2,048 races during his career. The poet Martial mentions him in a couple of encomiastic epigrams as an example of a charioteer who died prematurely; he laments that Lachesis (one of the Fates), when she tallied his career wins, must have thought that he was an old man, even though he had yet to attain the age of 30 when he died.

Martial elsewhere alludes to the great wealth which Scorpus amassed, claiming that as a charioteer, he could earn fifteen heavy bags of gold in only one hour of racing. The poet also describes a praetor bemoaning the fact that he would soon make a donation of over 100,000 sesterces to Scorpus and to another charioteer, Thallus.

Additionally, an inscription (*CIL* 6.10052) refers to a Scorpus — probably, but not certainly, the same Flavius Scorpus — and four of his winning horses: Pegasus, Elates, Andraemon and Cotynus.

SOURCE: Martial 4.67; 5.25; 10.50, 53, 74. Martial also mentions Scorpus briefly in 11.1, as a man whose charioteering prowess often inspired spectators to bet on him.

Florus. Roman charioteer, dates and place of origin unknown. The poignant inscription about Florus identifies him as a *bigarius infans*, child driver, one who early in life desired to race chariots, and whose life was shortened because of it. Some charioteers began their careers when they had barely reached their teens; presumably, Florus was one of these. SOURCE: *CIL* 6.10078.

Foot race. *See* Stade; Diaulos; Dolichos.

Four brother athletes. Timodemus, Cres, Crethus, Diocles, all sons of Clinus, dates and place of origin unknown. These four

Greek brothers won championships in the stade, wrestling, the pentathlon and boxing, respectively. SOURCE: *Greek Anthology* (Phalaecus) 13.5.

Furius Leptinus. Roman gladiator. See Calpenus Quintus.

Fuscus. Roman charioteer, 1st century A.D., place of origin unknown. Fuscus, a member of the Green faction, won 53 races in Rome, and several others at nearby locations; one of his 53 Roman victories was gained *revocatus*. The inscription pertaining to his career seems to indicate that he won a victory on his first day of racing, a feat which would have been quite unusual. He lived to the age of 24, and the plaque in his honor was erected in A.D. 35. In the inscription, Fuscus is identified as a *cursor*, a word literally meaning "runner"; by extension, it can also mean charioteer. Friedlaender identifies him as a foot racer, and it is known that foot races occasionally took place in the Circus Maximus (*see*, for example, Suetonius *Life of Augustus* 43). Harris calls him a charioteer, and this seems the more plausible interpretation, especially since the faction name appears adjacent to *cursor* in the inscription. SOURCE: *CIL* 6.33950. In his *Inscriptiones Latinae Selectae*, Dessau suggests that this inscription contains the earliest known reference to the Green faction (s.v. *ILS* 5278). Richmond Lattimore, in *Themes in Greek and Latin Epitaphs* (1962), quotes and translates the poignant epitaph of a Blue faction charioteer named Fuscus (*Carmina Latina Epigraphica* 500). The final words evoke particular interest: *Nemo tui similis*, "There was never anyone like you." (Literally: "No one [was] similar to you.")

Gerenus. Greek wrestler, dates unknown, Naucratis. A champion wrestler, Gerenus celebrated his Olympic triumph by overindulging in food and drink. When he resumed athletic training a few days later, his system was still so unbalanced by those excesses that he collapsed and died during a workout. SOURCE: Philostratus 54.

Glaucus. Greek boxer, late 6th or early 5th century, Carystus. Glaucus, a farmer by trade, one day made an innovative repair of a plowshare that had fallen from a plow: he hammered it back into place by striking it with his fist. His father, who observed the incident, entered him in the boxing competitions at the subsequent Olympiad. Glaucus, an inexperienced boxer, was on the verge of losing one of his matches when his father (or trainer) cried out: "Hit with the plowtouch!" Hearing these words, the son struck his opponent with redoubled force, and so attained the victory.

The onetime farmer went on to a distinguished career as a boxer, winning two Pythian championships, eight Nemean, and a like number at the Isthmian games. Contemporaries ranked him superior even to Polydeuces and Heracles in terms of strength and skill. It is said that Glaucus, far from disavowing such high praise, revelled in it, nor did he receive the divine retribution that one might anticipate in connection with an attitude so fraught with hubris. On the contrary, he enjoyed great fame and honor among the Greeks, as did Simonides, the epinicean poet who put into words those deity-challenging notions.

There is a story that a certain boxer, possibly Glaucus, refused to pay the full sum of money he owed to Simonides, who had written an ode in honor of his boxing prowess. It seems that Simonides had included in the ode a digression in praise of Castor and Pollux; the boxer suggested to Simonides that he collect the rest of the money from them. Later, during a banquet held in the boxer's honor, Simonides (who had been invited) was told that two young men waiting outside wished to speak with him. When he left the banquet hall in search of them, he found no one. His absence at that moment was propitious, however, for while he was away, the roof collapsed and the entire company of revellers was killed.

SOURCES: Cicero *Concerning the Orator* 2.86 (352–353); Demosthenes *Concerning the Crown* 319, where Demosthenes notes that the Olympic boxing winner in 360, Philammon, won not because he surpassed the long-dead Glaucus in strength, but because he outfought his contemporary opponents. A similar observation is made by Aeschines *Against Ctesiphon* 189; Dio Crysostom 78.20; Lucian *Essays in Portraiture Defended* 19; Pausanias 6.10.1–4; Philostratus 20; Quintilian 11.2; Simonides *Greek Lyric* 2.30.

Glaucus. Roman gladiator *(retiarius)*, unknown, Mutina. Glaucus fought eight bouts, the final one resulting in his death at age 23. His epitaph contains the curious message: "I warn you, each one, to take control of his own destiny, and not have faith in Nemesis. Thus was I taken in." Some gladiators viewed the goddess Nemesis with a healthy respect as an avenging deity who might cause them either to be spared or to be killed, depending on her particular whim. By paying homage to her, so they thought, they might gain her favor. Glaucus, evidently a Nemesis worshipper, warned his gladiatorial colleagues against a practice which obviously failed to protect him. SOURCE: *CIL* 5.3466.

Glycon. Greek pankratiast, dates unknown, Pergamum. A sepulchral epigram on Glycon calls him the broad-footed second coming of Atlas, a man undefeated in pankration contests in Italy, Greece and Asia. Only Hades could manage to throw him. SOURCE: *Greek Anthology* (Antipater or Philippus) 7.692.

Gold faction. *See* Faction.

Gorgus. Greek pentathlete/diaulos racer/hoplite racer, dates unknown, Elis. Gorgus strung together pentathlon victories at four (presumably consecutive) Olympiads, a feat which had never been accomplished up to Pausanias' time (2nd century A.D.). Gorgus also won Olympic championships in the diaulos and the armored race. SOURCE: Pausanias 6.15.9.

Gracchus. Roman gladiator *(retiarius)*, probably 2nd century A.D., place of origin unknown. The satirist Juvenal, in writing of Gracchus, provides some details about the costuming and accoutrements of *retiarii:* no helmet, shield or sword; a golden tunic; protective padding for the shoulder. Juvenal also refers to the uncovered faces of the *retiarii*, which made them easily recognizable to the arena patrons. Gladiators were generally social outcasts; should a wellborn Roman citizen volunteer for gladiatorial service (not unheard of), he would undoubtedly have preferred to fight in one of the other classifications in order to preserve some semblance of anonymity.

In the particular bout which Juvenal describes, Gracchus was matched with the usual opponent for a *retiarius:* a *secutor.* SOURCE: Juvenal 8.199–210. In 2.143ff, Juvenal claims that Gracchus was an aristocratic Roman, of nobler birth than some of the city's most well-known families.

Green; Greens; Green faction. *See* Faction.

Gymnasion. (Latinized form *gymnasium.*) A large, usually rectangular, Greek structure featuring running tracks, dressing areas, meeting rooms, and a prominent, centrally placed, open-air arena for use by pentathletes and possibly heavy eventers. The word ultimately derives from the Greek *gymnos* ("naked"), a reference to athletes competing unclothed.

These buildings sometimes served as social and intellectual centers; Plato's Academy and Aristotle's Lyceum were both *gymnasia*.

Halteres. *See* Long jump.

Heavy event. A term sometimes applied in Greek sports to boxing, wrestling and the pankration, it arose from the dominance of those three events by the heaviest, bulkiest competitors.

Heavy eventer. *See* Heavy event.

Hecatomnus. Greek stade/diaulos/hoplite racer, 1st century, Miletus. In the 177th Olympiad (72), Hecatomnus won championships in all three of the events listed above. SOURCES: Eusebius 211; Photius 190 [97].

Hedea. Greek chariot racer in armor/stade racer, mid–1st century A.D., Tralles Caesarea. Hedea, sister of Tryphosa (q.v.) and Dionysia (q.v.) won the chariot race at the Isthmian games and the stade at Nemea and Sicyon. SOURCE: *IAG* 63.

Hellanicus. Greek boxer. *See* Alcaenetus.

Hellanodicae. The Elean-appointed judges at the Greek Olympic games.

Heraclides. Greek boxer, late 1st century A.D., Alexandria. Heraclides won an *akoniti* boxing championship at the 218th Olympiad (A.D. 93). The only man who might have provided him with a serious challenge, Apollonius, had arrived at Olympia too late to register for boxing, and so was excluded from the competitions. Apollonius claimed that he had been delayed at sea by contrary winds, but Heraclides countered that Apollonius had dallied at a money festival. Apollonius was so infuriated by that testimony that he strapped on the *himantes* and attacked Heraclides, even though Heraclides had already been declared the boxing winner. For this offense, Apollonius was heavily fined. SOURCE: Pausanias 5.21. 12–14.

Heras. Greek pankratiast, [1st century A.D.], Laodicaea. The description of Heras' physique — bull-bellied, thick-limbed, a second Atlas — might apply to any successful pankratiast. Heras won crowns at the Olympic, Pythian and Isthmian games, as well as championships in festivals at Smyrna, Argos, Pergamum and Actium. He claimed — no doubt with a touch of exaggeration — that his total number of victories was larger than the number of grains of sand in the Libyan desert. SOURCE: *Greek Anthology* (Philippus) 16.52.

Hercules. Greek boxer. *See* Diognetus.

Hermeros. Roman gladiator. *See* Petraites.

Hermogenes. Greek foot racer, 1st century A.D., Xanthus. Hermogenes won a total of eight Olympic foot race championships, including triumphs in the stade at the 215th and 217th Olympiads (81, 89 A.D.). The Greeks nicknamed him "Hippos," horse. SOURCES: Eusebius 215; Pausanias 6.13.3.

Hermogenes. Greek stade racer, dates unknown, Antioch. Hermogenes won stade races at the Isthmian and Nemean games. The epigrammatist adds that Hermogenes ran like Hermes, and also incidentally notes that he defeated nine other contestants, probably at Nemea. SOURCE: *Greek Anthology* (Philippus) 6.259.

Herodorus. Event and dates unknown, Megara. Herodorus, a small Greek man (barely over five feet tall), had a prodigious appetite, supposedly, it was said, downing six loaves of bread, twenty pounds of meat and two pitchers of wine per day. He served as a trumpeter for the Megarian army, a post for which he was well suited, since he could sound two trumpets simultaneously. According to Athenaeus, he was *periodonikes* an astounding ten times, but there is no reference to the event in which he established this remarkable record. Given his dietary habits, one would assume that he was a heavy eventer. SOURCES: Athenaeus 10.414E; 415A; Pollux 4.89.

Herodotus. Greek chariot racer, 5th century, Thebes. Herodotus won charioteering victories at the Olympic and Pythian games. He also triumphed at the Isthmian games, where he drove the chariot himself. (A rather unusual occurrence; *see* Equestrian events.) SOURCE: Pindar *Isthmian* 1.

Hierax. Roman charioteer. *See* Cresces.

Hieronymus. Greek pentathlete. *See* Tisamenus.

Himantes. Strips of braided oxhide which Greek boxers wrapped around their knuckles; the ancient form of boxing gloves.

Hippodrome. *See* Equestrian events.

Hippomachus. Greek boxer (boys'), dates unknown, Elis. Hippomachus achieved the rather unusual distinction of winning his Olympic boxing crown against three opponents without sustaining injury or even any blows. Source: Pausanias 6.12.6.

Hipposthenes. Greek wrestler, 7th century, Sparta. Hipposthenes won the boys' wrestling the first year (632) in which it was an Olympic event. He went on to triumph in the men's division in four of the next five Olympiads. In Sparta, his athletic prowess brought him the sort of veneration generally reserved for deities. Sources: Eusebius 197; Pausanias 3.15.7; 5.8.9.

Hoplite race. *See* Armored race.

Hoplomachus. A kind of heavily armed Roman gladiator; little is known about the specifics of the *hoplomachus'* weaponry or armor.

Horse racing. *See* Equestrian events.

Hypenus. Greek diaulos racer, 8th century, Pisa. The program of events at Olympia was expanded for the first time in the 14th Olympiad (724), with the addition of the diaulos, won by Hypenus. Sources: Eusebius 195; Pausanias 5.8.6; Philostratus 12.

Hysmon. Greek pentathlete, [4th century], Elis. Hysmon, sickly as a child, turned to athletic training as a way to improve his health. His regimen was so effective that when he reached manhood, he decided to enter the crown festivals, competing successfully in the pentathlon in both the Olympic and Nemean games. Like other Eleans, however, he refused to take part in the Isthmian games. *See* Timon. SOURCE: Pausanias 6.3.9–10.

Iatrocles. Greek boxer, 1st century A.D., place of origin unknown. Iatrocles was one of the most persistent opponents of the invincible Melancomas (q.v.). He was the only man who could compete on nearly equal terms with Melancomas, and yet he never defeated him. When Melancomas died unexpectedly, Iatrocles felt a certain perverse joy at the event, for he realized that he could very likely assume his rival's place as the best boxer of the time. SOURCE: Dio Chrysostom 28.4.

Ibaton. Greek wrestler, late 8th century, Sparta. Ibaton was the wrestling winner in the first year that it was an Olympic event (708). SOURCE: Eusebius 195.

Iccus. Greek boxer. *See* Cleomedes.

Iccus. Greek pentathlete, dates unknown, Tarentum. The winner of an Olympic championship in the pentathlon, Iccus later gained fame as a skilled trainer of athletes. He exhibited a high degree of self-discipline in his quest for Olympic glory, including sexual abstinence while preparing for the games. SOURCES: Aelian *On Animals* 6.1; *Various Histories* 11.3 (where he is wrongly identified as a wrestler); Lucian *How to Write History* 35; Pausanias 6.10.5; Plato *Laws* 8.839E, 840D; *Protagoras* 316D.

Incitatus. Roman charioteer, 1st century A.D., place of origin unknown. Martial briefly alludes to Incitatus in a couple of epigrams, as a charioteer known for attracting bettors at the races; and as a man who is rich enough to wear a scarlet robe, while a contemporary poet can afford only a dark and (by implication) cheap one. SOURCE: Martial 10.76; 11.1. Incitatus was also the name of one of the emperor Caligula's favorite chariot race horses. He ordered for Incitatus a marble stall, an ivory stable, purple blankets, a bejeweled collar, and even a house replete with servants and furniture. It was also said that he intended to nominate Incitatus for a consulship. *See* Suetonius *Life of Caligula* 55.; cf. Dio Cassius 59.14.

Isthmian games. Probably the most commercialized of the four crown festivals, the biennial Isthmian games were held near the Greek city of Corinth.

Javelin throw. One of the five events of the Greek pentathlon. Ancient throwing techniques differed little from the modern, with the exception that in antiquity, the thrower wound a leather thong around one or more of his fingers and the shaft of the javelin. The purpose of this is unknown, but it is likely that the thong (which unraveled at the point of release) was thought to impart a tighter spiral to the javelin in flight, and thus a truer and longer throw.

Kalpe. *See* Equestrian events.

Lacerta. Roman charioteer, 1st century A.D., place of origin unknown. Juvenal uses Lacerta, a Red faction charioteer, as an example of the tremendous wealth which Roman charioteers could amass. In Lacerta's case, that wealth amounted to 100 times the net worth of a successful lawyer. SOURCE: Juvenal 7. 112–114. The name of the charioteer Caius Annius Lacerta appears in an inscription (*CIL* 15.6250), but it seems likely that Juvenal's Lacerta was a different individual.

Ladas. Greek dolichos racer, dates and place of origin unknown. Reputedly the fastest runner of his day, Ladas supposedly was so light on his feet that he left no imprint in the sand on which he ran, and so swift a runner that he seemed to fly over the track. A stadium in Arcadia where he practiced was later named in his honor. He apparently fell ill and died on his way home following one of his Olympic triumphs.

Ladas appears occasionally in Roman literature, where his swiftness of foot reached legendary proportions. Catullus (55.25), Martial (2.86; 10.100) and Seneca (*Letters* 85.4) all refer to him, and in all cases as the epitome of running speed. Only the morose Juvenal has a negative comment, acerbically remarking that Ladas would rather have had the rich man's gout than a worthless olive wreath (13.97–99.) ADDITIONAL SOURCES: *Greek Anthology* (Anonymous) 16.53–54; Solinus 1.96.

Lampis. Greek pentathlete, late 8th century, Sparta. Lampis earned the crown in the pentathlon in the 18th Olympiad (708), the first year in which pentathlon competitions were held at the Olympics. SOURCES: Eusebius 195; Pausanias 5.8.7; Philostratus 12.

Lanista. A Roman gladiatorial owner or manager. The term is frequently mistranslated as "trainer"; in fact, the word for a trainer of gladiators was *doctor.*

Leon. Greek stade racer. *See* Eupolemus.

Leonidas. Greek stade/diaulos/dolichos racer, 2nd century, Rhodes. Leonidas, called by Pausanias the "most outstanding runner," was *triastes* at four consecutive Olympiads (164, 160, 156, 152), the only man in Olympic history to accomplish this. Sources: Dio Chrysostom 31.126; Eusebius 209; Pausanias 6.13.4; Philostratus 33.

Leontiscus. Greek pankratiast, late 4th century, Messana (Sicily). A two-time Olympic champion, Leontiscus once enjoyed a dalliance with a certain Mania, with whom he lived as if she were his wife. To his dismay, he discovered that she was simultaneously entertaining another pankratiast, Antenor (whose name also appears in the Lycaean victor list as the pankration winner for 320; *see* Appendix). When he confronted her, she replied that she had merely wished to find out what two champion pankratiasts could do, blow for blow, in a setting other than the athletic field.

Sources: Athenaeus 13.578F; Pausanias 6.4.3. In his monumental book on the Olympic winners, Moretti indicates that the Leontiscus mentioned by Athenaeus (13.578F) and Pausanias' Leontiscus (6.4.3) were two different athletes. He makes this distinction (apparently) on the basis of the events in which the two competed: Athenaeus' Leontiscus was a pankratiast; Pausanias', a wrestler. Both men (if indeed there were two) lived in the late 4th century; hence, chronology is not a factor.

Pausanias states that Leontiscus, unable to master the throws required of wrestler, resorted to the technique perfected by Sostratus (q.v.): bending back his opponent's fingers, until presumably the opponent yielded. However, victory in wrestling was determined not by pain-induced capitulation but by causing one's opponent to fall backwards onto the ground. It is difficult to see how the finger-bending strategy would facilitate this.

It is more probable that the Leontiscus mentioned in Pausanias was a pankratiast, not a wrestler. Although a wide variety of holds were permitted in wrestling, it seems implausible that he would have achieved distinction in the event using a technique far more suited to the requirements of the pankration.

Finally, given that: (1) Athenaeus' and Pausanias' Leontiscus were contemporaries, and (2) both were (most likely) pankratiasts, it would follow that they were indeed one man. In any case, that is the reason for combining the testimony of Athenaeus and Pausanias into one entry.

Leucinas. Greek boxer/pankratiast, 1st century, Thebes. Leucinas' feat of winning the boys' boxing and men's pankration at the same festival (at Oropus) was rare indeed; this kind of divisional crossover is unattested at the crown festivals, and must have been most unusual even in the localized athletic meetings. SOURCE: *IG* 7.417. (*IG* 7.420 records an Aretippus of Sparta, who won championships at the festival of Oropus in both the youths' stade and men's diaulos.)

Lichas. Greek chariot racer, 5th century, Sparta. Lichas entered a chariot in the Olympic games of 416 under the aegis of Thebes, since Sparta had been excluded from the festival that year. His team won the race, but since an Olympic competitor was expected to represent only his native city, the authorities at Elis ordered Lichas to be scourged, and the victory credited not to him, but to the Theban people. This incident sparked a brief war between Sparta and Elis; afterwards, Lichas set up his own victory monument, although the Eleans still refused to acknowledge his victory.

Lichas' father, Arcesilas (q.v.), won two — apparently legitimate — Olympic charioteering crowns.

SOURCES: Pausanias 6.2.2–3; Plutarch *Life of Cimon* 10; Thucydides 5.50 (Thucydides also refers to Lichas' activities during the Peloponnesian War at several points in Book 8); Xenophon *Hellenica* 3.2. (Xenophon adds that Lichas was an old man when he was scourged.)

Long jump. One of the five events of the Greek pentathlon. The ancient long jump was identical to the modern except that ancient jumpers carried metal or stone weights *(halteres)* in each hand. Their reason for so doing is unknown, although according to Aristotle, the explanation was simple enough: long jumpers believed that they could jump farther using the weights.

Ludia. The wife, mistress or female devotee of a Roman gladiator.

Ludus. A Roman gladiatorial school. There were many *ludi* scattered throughout Italy and elsewhere. Perhaps the most famous was the Ludus Magnus in Rome.

Ludus Magnus. *See* Ludus.

Lycus. Roman gladiator *(murmillo)*, dates and place of origin unknown. Lycus fought four times. It is recorded in the inscription that he was left-handed, apparently a special advantage given that some categories of gladiators wore armor only on the left side of their bodies as protection against opponents who were usually right-handed. SOURCE: *CIL* 6.10196. (*See also* Apollonius.)

Lygdamis. Greek pankratiast, mid–7th century, Syracuse. Lygdamis won the pankration at the 33rd Olympiad (648), the first year in which pankration competitions were held at the Olympics. The Syracusans claimed that Lygdamis was as big as Heracles of Thebes, although Pausanias was dubious of the claim. SOURCES: Eusebius 197; Pausanias 5.8.8; Philostratus 12.

Macedo. Roman gladiator (Thracian), dates unknown, Alexandria. There is nothing unusual about Macedo's epitaph except the statement that his monument was commissioned by the *armatura Thraecum universa*, the whole armed band of Thracian gladiators. This suggests that a certain amount of camaraderie existed in the rough and brutal world of a Roman gladiator. Macedo lived to the age of 20 years, seven months and 12 days. SOURCE: *CIL* 6.10197.

Mandragenes. Greek pankratiast, dates unknown, Magnesia. Mandragenes' prowess in the pankration was due to a letter which his trainer had written to his mother. In the letter, he instructed her to believe any rumors she may hear of her son's death, but to disbelieve reports of his defeat. This missive motivated Mandragenes to put forth his best effort, for he wished neither to discredit his trainer nor to disappoint his mother. SOURCE: Philostratus 23.

Marion. Greek wrestler/pankratiast. *See* Straton.

Melancomas. Greek boxer, 1st century A.D., Caria. The boxer Melancomas was undefeated in crown festival competition. Despite the brutality of the event in which he competed, he was handsome to look at, with a face as unmarked by cuts or scars as that of a foot racer.

He was able to maintain his facial features because of the style of boxing he developed. He neither struck an opponent — an act which he considered cowardly and indicative of a lack of stamina — nor did he allow himself to be struck. Rather, he wore out his rivals with feints and constant motion, until they became so fatigued that they could not continue. This strategy worked even against the strongest and most skilled boxers of the time. *See also* Iatrocles.

Dio Chrysostom composed a eulogy for Melancomas; excerpts are quoted in *Special Essay 5*, page 112–114.
SOURCE: Dio Chrysostom 28.5–10; 29.

Melesias. Greek wrestler (boys') pankratiast, 5th century, Athens. Melesias won championships at Nemea in boys' wrestling, and later the men's pankration, but he gained greater fame as the trainer of many successful heavy eventers. By 460, his protégés had won a total of 30 championships. SOURCE: Pindar *Olympian 8; Nemean 4, 6.*

Men's division. Competitions at the Greek crown festivals were offered in a men's division (applying to athletes older than age 18), and a boys' division. At many other festivals, three age groups were recognized: men's, boys', and young men's, or youths' (presumably ages 18 to 21). One early 20th century scholar, Th. Klee, suggested that some athletic meetings had as many as five age divisions.

Metae. In Roman chariot racing, three large conical projections located at both ends of the *spina*, and used as turning posts.

Metrodorus. Greek wrestler/pankratiast, 2nd century, Athens. Metrodorus was one of the premier heavy eventers of the 2nd century. His career is attested in a fragmentary inscription found in Athens, and a better preserved inscription discovered in Delos. According to the Delian inscription, he won championships at many prestigious festivals, including two at Olympia (one in wrestling, one in the pankration), three at Nemea (two in wrestling, one in the pankration) and two at the Panathenaea (both in the pankration). He also triumphed at Eleusinia, Soteria, Lycaea, Heraclea, Delos and elsewhere. SOURCE: *IAG 51.*

Metrodotus. Roman charioteer, dates and place of origin unknown. Metrodotus, a Blue faction charioteer, despised the Greens so intensely that he kept a green-colored table at his home as a constant reminder of his hatred for the Green faction. SOURCE: *Greek Anthology* (Anonymous) 11.344.

Milesian runner [his name is missing from the inscription]. Greek stade/diaulos/armored racer, 1st century A.D. A lengthy inscription records this athlete's many noteworthy deeds. He claims, among other feats, to have won the men's stade, diaulos and armored race at the same Pythiad; and to have been the first man in history to win a similar triple, same day championship at Nemea. He also won races at numerous other festivals, including those held at Actium, Plataea, Argos, Rhodes and Athens. SOURCE: *IAG 59. See also* Harris' translation and commentary in *Greek Athletes and Athletics*, pages 126–127.

Milo. Greek wrestler, flourished 536–508, Croton. Milo attained fame in wrestling by winning six times each at the Olympic and Pythian games, ten times at the Isthmian games, and nine times at the Nemean. He was four times *periodonikes.* According to Pliny, he owed his success to his habit of carrying with him some lucky stones called *alectoriae* (stones found in the gizzards of roosters.)

Occasionally, potential opponents for noted heavy eventers like Milo could not be found; in such cases, the victory would be awarded by default *(akoniti).* This happened to Milo at one of the Olympiads. However, as he stepped forward to claim his crown, he slipped and fell, whereupon the crowd demanded that he not be awarded the victory. But Milo retorted that wrestling involved three falls; he challenged any among the spectators to cause him to fall a second time. Not surprisingly, no one volunteered.

In addition to his athletic excellence, he was something of a showman, delighting in tests of skill and strength. He would grasp a pomegranate loosely enough so as not to damage the fruit, and yet so tightly that no one could uncurl his fingers. He enjoyed standing on a greased discus and challenging all comers to attempt to dislodge him. He would tie a leather cord around his head and then, by holding his breath and thereby causing the veins in his head to expand, burst the cord. He liked to hold his hand out, perpendicular to the ground with the little finger at the bottom, and then challenge onlookers to try to bend or pull his little finger out of place. No one ever succeeded in so doing.

It is said that on one occasion, Milo happened upon a shepherd by the name of Titormus. When Milo took note of Titormus' imposing physique, he challenged him to a contest of strength. Titormus demurred, but Milo persisted, until at length the herdsman agreed. He walked down to the bank of a nearby river, dragged back a large boulder, lifted it up, carried it some fifty feet, and finally tossed it. But when Milo attempted to duplicate those feats, he could barely move the rock.

On another occasion, Milo's hometown of Croton had gone to war against the neighboring community of Sybaris. Wearing his Olympic wreaths, and attired like Heracles, with club and lion skin, Milo led the charge against the enemy troops and routed them.

Like many oversized athletes throughout history, Milo had a prodigious appetite, reportedly downing twenty pounds of meat and bread and three pitchers of wine at a single sitting. He is said to have once carried a four-year-old bull around the stadium, and then to have butchered it and consumed it in its entirety; and to have engaged in an ox-eating contest with Titormus. Another time, at a festival in honor of Zeus, he lifted on his shoulders a four-year-old steer, paraded with it among the festival-goers, and then supposedly butchered and ate it. Nor were these the only occasions on which Milo hoisted bovines onto his shoulders. According to Quintilian, he trained by carrying a calf in such a manner. As the calf grew, so presumably did Milo's strength, for he was still able to carry it when it had become a bull.

Milo's death occurred one day in a forest when he happened to come upon a fallen oak tree left partially split by some lumberers. Placing his hands and feet in the cleft, he attempted to complete the split himself. In this effort he was unsuccessful: his appendages became wedged in the log. Unable to free himself, he was subsequently devoured by wild animals.

SOURCES: Aelian *Various History* 2.24; 12.22; Athenaeus 10.412E, F; 413A; Diodorus Siculus 12.9; Eusebius 201; *Greek Anthology* (Anonymous) 11.316; (Simonides) 16.24, where he is credited with seven Olympic victories instead of six; Aulus Gellius 15.16; Lucian *Essays in Portraiture Defended* 19; *Herodotus* 8; Pausanias 6.14.5–9; Philostratus *Life of Apollonius* 4.28; Pliny the Elder 7.83; 37.54; Quintilian 1.9; Simonides *Greek Lyric* 2.185; Strabo 6.1.

Mnesibulus. Greek stade/hoplite racer, 2nd century A.D., Elatea. Mnesibulus won both the stade and the hoplite events at the

235th Olympiad (A.D. 161). His hometown erected a statue of him, located, fittingly, on the Street of the Runner. SOURCES: *IG* 10.1146; Pausanias 10.34.5.

Monocostelus. Roman gladiator *(murmillo)*, dates and place of origin unknown. The brief inscription pertaining to Monocostelus suggests that he participated in 40 matches in his career, an astoundingly high total. SOURCE: *AE* 1971 (263).

Moschus. Greek boxer (boys'), late 3rd century, Colophon. By winning the boys' boxing at the 145th Olympiad (200), Moschus became the only athlete ever to earn the title *periodonikes* in that event. [Presumably his victory at Olympia completed the circuit.] SOURCE: Eusebius 209.

Munera. *See* Munus.

Munus. (Pl. *munera;* literal meaning: "gift.") The standard Latin word for gladiatorial show. Its connection with gift giving comes from the time when shows were given to the populace by politicians eager to gain favor and name recognition with potential voters. The usual term for a sponsor of Roman gladiatorial shows was the derivative, *munerarius.*

Murmillo. (Sometimes spelled *myrmillo.*) A kind of Roman gladiator. The costuming and armor of *murmillones* are not well attested, but the evidence seems to indicate that they were helmeted and equipped with swords or clubs.

Musclosus. Roman charioteer (not to be confused with Pompeius Musclosus, q.v.), dates unknown, Tuscus. Musclosus won 682 races during his career, including three as a member of the White faction, five with the Greens and two with the Blues. The other 672 all came while he was a wearer of the Red. Apuleia Verecunda, his wife, dedicated his monument. SOURCE: *CIL* 6.10063.

Myrmillo. *See* Murmillo.

[Name not extant.] Roman charioteer, early 2nd century A.D., place of origin unknown. This unnamed charioteer apparently died on August 20, in the year 108, at the age of 25. He spent his entire career with the Blue faction, with whom he compiled the following statistics: In quadrigae, he won 47 races; he came in second 136(?) times (the number is fragmentary in the inscription), and third on 146 occasions. In bigae, he recorded nine firsts, eight seconds and eight thirds. He also gained two wins *adgente quadrigam*, two more *revocatus* and one *instauratiam*.

A statistical incongruity occurs near the end of the inscription, where the charioteer claims to have placed either first, second or third in 354 races. However, the sum of the numbers mentioned above (47, 120, 146, 9, 8, 8, 2, 2, 1) is only 343. Some editors would amend the fragmentary 120 to 131 to account for the discrepancy.

The (certainly funerary) monument on which the inscription appears was erected by one Crispina Meroe, presumably the driver's widow. Source: *CIL* 6.10055.

Nemean games. One of the four Greek crown festivals, the biennial Nemean games were held near the site on the Peloponnesus where Heracles supposedly killed and skinned the Nemean Lion, the first of his famed Twelve Labors.

Nero. *See* Special Essay 3, pages 108–109.

Nicander. Greek stade/diaulos racer, late 4th/early 3rd century, Elis. Nicander won two Olympic championships in the diaulos, and six more foot racing crowns at the Nemean games. Source: Pausanias 6.16.5.

Nicasylus. Greek wrestler, dates unknown, Rhodes. Nicasylus attempted to enter the boys' wrestling at Olympia, but was adjudged too old — he was eighteen at the time — and so he competed in the men's division, and won. He also won at the subsequent Nemean and Isthmian games, but died at the age of 20, before returning to Rhodes and a triumphant homecoming. Source: Pausanias 6.14.1–2.

Nicocles. Greek boxer. *See* Cleander.

Nicoladas. Greek foot racer (probably the stade), late 6th or early 5th century, Corinth. Nicoladas won races at many festivals, including those at Tegea, Aegina, Epidaurus, Thebes and Megara.

He also won twice at Lycaea, four times at Pellana, three times each at the Nemean and Isthmian games, once at the Pythian games, and five times at the Panathenaic games. His victories at the Panathenaic games earned him sixty jars of expensive Athenian olive oil. At Phlius, he performed a rare feat: a double victory (pentathlon and foot race). SOURCE: *Greek Anthology* (Simonides) 13.19.

Nicomachus. Greek chariot racer. *See* Xenocrates.

Nicon. Greek pankratiast, early 3rd century, Boeotia. Nicon won two Olympic pankration championships, including one at the 121st Olympiad (296), in addition to two triumphs at the Pythian games, four at the Nemean and four at the Isthmian. SOURCE: *Papyrus Oxyrhynchus* 20.2082.

Nicostratus. Greek wrestler/pankratiast. *See* Straton.

Occupavit et vicit. (Literal meaning: "he seized [the lead] and won.") A Roman chariot racing strategy in which the driver tried to gain the lead at the outset, and hold it throughout the race.

Odontophorus. (Literal meaning: "tooth-bearing.") A kind of necklace made of teeth, and sometimes worn by Greek race horses, perhaps as a good luck charm.

Oebotas. Greek stade racer, 8th century, Dyme. Oebotas won the stade at the sixth Olympiad (756). However, a statue honoring his victory was not erected until the 80th Olympiad (460). The reason for the delay is given by Pausanias as follows: Oebotas was the first man from Achaea (the region in which Dyme was located) to win an Olympic championship. However, he received no prizes or acclaim from his fellow Achaeans for his accomplishment. Because of this slight, he pronounced a curse that all future Achaean athletes be denied Olympic victories. As Pausanias puts it, some god must have been listening, because centuries passed and no Achaean triumphed at Olympia.

Eventually, however, a delegation of frustrated Achaeans was sent to Apollo's oracle at Delphi to learn the reason for this dearth of crowns. Having discovered the cause of their troubles, they returned home, erected the statue of Oebotas, and paid him the requisite posthumous honors. The curse was lifted, and not long after, Sostratus (q.v.) of Pellana in Achaea won the boys' stade race.

Pausanias adds that it was still the custom in his own day for Olympia-bound Achaean athletes to offer sacrifices to Oebotas, and, if they won, to place a wreath on his statue at Olympia. SOURCES: Eusebius 195; Pausanias 6.3.8; 7.17.6–7; 8.17.13–14.

Olympae. Roman charioteer. *See* Cresces.

Olympic games. The oldest and most prestigious of the four Greek crown festivals, the quadrennial Olympic games attracted athletes and spectators from every corner of the Greek world. The other crown festivals, and very likely other athletic meets as well, were patterned after the Olympic games.

Olympicus. Greek boxer, probably 1st century A.D., place of origin unknown. Olympicus, like most human beings, once possessed a nose, chin, forehead and ears, but after taking up boxing as a profession, he lost them all, becoming so disfigured and unrecognizable that he was denied a share of his family inheritance. It was suggested to him that he never look into a reflecting pool of water, for if he did so, the ugliness of his countenance would kill him. SOURCE: *Greek Anthology* (Lucillius) 11.75, 76.

Olyntheus. Greek stade racer, 7th century, Sparta. Olyntheus won the stade race at the 38th Olympiad (628), lost his title to Rhipsolaus of Sparta in 624, and then regained it in 620. SOURCE: Eusebius 199.

Onomastus. Greek boxer, early 7th century, Smyrna. Boxing was added to the Olympic program in 688, and Onomastus was the first winner. He was also instrumental in establishing the regulations for boxing. SOURCES: Eusebius 195; Pausanias 5.8.7; Philostratus 12.

Orhippus. (sometimes spelled Orrhippus or Orsippus). Greek stade racer, 8th century, Megara. Orhippus, Olympic stade winner for 720, is said by Pausanias to have been the first athlete to compete nude, albeit by accident: his loincloth supposedly fell off while he was in the midst of running. Other athletes, observing the success of Orhippus *au naturel*, adopted the custom, believing that they, too, could run faster unclad. (A logical conclusion; athletes have always tended to resist wearing of apparel or even protective equipment which they thought might impede their ability to compete.) After his death, he was buried near the first recorded stade winner, Coroebus (q.v.). *See also* Acanthus. SOURCES: *IG* 7.52; Pausanias 1.44.1.

Orsippus. *See* Orhippus.

Pacideianus. Roman gladiator, 1st century B.C. or earlier, place of origin unknown. Pacideianus was by some accounts the best gladiator by far in human history. The violence and ferocity with which he fought are illustrated by his method of preparing himself to meet his opponent: "I'll first take his blow in my face*; I'll stick my sword into the idiot's stomach and lungs. I hate the man; I fight with fury. . . . To this extreme am I swept away by passionate anger and hatred for the man, and by my own rage."

Pacideianus' contemporary Aeserninus, a Samnite, was evidently considered nearly his equal, and a man strong enough for any opponent. It appears that Aeserninus and Pacideianus were occasionally matched against each other.

SOURCES: Cicero *Concerning the Best Kind of Orators 17; Letters to his Brother Quintus* 3.4.; *Tusculan Disputations* 4.48, where Cicero mentions Pacideianus as an example of a gladiator who cannot fight effectively unless he has first worked himself up to a state of blind rage; Horace *Satires* 2.7.97; *Remains of Old Latin* (LCL) Vol. III, pages 56, 58 [Lucilius]. *Cicero (*Tusculan Disputations* 4.41) asserts that gladiators often preferred to absorb blows rather than to avoid them, for avoiding blows was apparently considered cowardly.

Paeanius. Wrestler. *See* Caprus.

Paegniarius. A kind of Roman gladiator who apparently performed only at the mock bouts *(prolusiones)* preceding the serious matches.

Pagondas. Greek chariot racer, early 7th century, Thebes. Pagondas won the crown in four-horse chariot racing in 680, the first year for that event in the Olympics. SOURCE: Pausanias 5.8.7.

Palaestra. A Greek building resembling a *gymnasion*, but usually smaller, and perhaps more specialized, as the etymology of the word (from *pale*, "wrestling"), indicates. At Olympia the *palaestra* was directly adjacent to the *gymnasion*.

Pankration. A violent Greek event combining features of boxing and wrestling. In the pankration, all manner of hitting, kicking, tripping, hair pulling, strangling, and twisting of arms, legs and fingers was permitted. Only gouging and biting were prohibited. As in boxing, the match ended when one athlete yielded/or became too exhausted or dazed to continue.

Pantacles. Greek stade/diaulos(?) racer, early 7th century, Athens. Pantacles won the stade at two consecutive Olympiads (696, 692). He was the first Olympic athlete to successfully defend his stade championship. SOURCE: Eusebius 195. A fragmentary inscription (*IG* 2.2326) indicates that he may also have been a champion diaulos runner.

Paraballon. Greek diaulos racer, [3rd century], Elis. Paraballon was not only an Olympic champion, but also a quasi-historian: he inscribed the names of other Olympic winners on the walls of the gymnasium there. SOURCE: Pausanias 6.6.3.

Paris. Roman gladiator *(murmillo?)*, 1st century A.D., place of origin unknown. Paris' name appears in a Pompeian wall poster which advertises an upcoming series of five gladiatorial shows. Paris, apparently a well known gladiator of the day, was presumably scheduled to compete in all five shows. (The frequency of his performances supports the contention, proposed in the introductory section, about the relatively low gladiatorial mortality rate; most *munerarii* depended on big-name gladiators to increase attendance at shows.) SOURCE: *CIL* 4.1179.

Pedibus ad quadrigam. (Literal meaning: "on foot toward the chariot.") A term from Roman chariot racing. Although its exact application is uncertain, it probably referred to a race in which the charioteers covered part of the course on foot. Some authorities believe that the foot race occurred at the end of the chariot race, with the driver dismounting at some point on the track and running to the finish line, similar, perhaps to the Greek *kalpe* (q.v.). It is difficult to envision the practicality of this, however, given the likelihood that the running charioteers would be competing for space with chariots whose drivers had not yet reached the dismount point. It makes far more sense — both logistically and grammatically — to suggest that the foot race occurred at the *beginning;* perhaps the drivers were required to run some distance toward their chariots before commencing the horse-drawn portion of the race.

Pentathlon. A Greek event consisting of five separate contests: the long jump, the discus, the javelin throw, a foot race (probably the stade), and wrestling. The long jump, discus and javelin throws were never independent events, but were conducted only as a part of the pentathlon. It is not known how overall victory in the pentathlon was determined, although many ingenious theories have been postulated by modern scholars.

Pericles. Greek foot racer, dates and place of origin unknown. In one of the races which he entered, Pericles moved so slowly that it was impossible for an onlooker to determine if he were running or sitting. While the winner of the race was receiving his crown, Pericles was still at the starting line. SOURCE: *Greek Anthology* (Anonymous) 11.86.

Periodonikes. (Literal meaning: "winner all around the circuit.") An honorary title applied to a Greek athlete who had won championships at all four crown festivals in succession.

Petraites. Roman gladiator, 1st century A.D., place of origin unknown. Petraites is mentioned twice by Petronius in the *Satyricon:* once (52.3), when Trimalchio boasts of an expensively engraved cup in his possession, which showed Petraites paired with another gladiator, Hermeros; and again (71.6), when he demands that all the fights of Petraites be portrayed on his funerary monument.

Variant spellings of the name (Tetraites, Petrahes) appear on a number of glass cups depicting gladiatorial activity. This, in turn, has triggered a rather lively debate about the correct identity of the epigraphical Petraites vis-à-vis the Petronian Petraites, the possible connection between the names Petraites, Tetraites and Petrahes, and the implications of all this for the dating of the *Satyricon*. (For a complete review of the evidence and the resultant debate, the reader should consult H. T. Rowell's article "The Gladiator Petraites and the Date of the *Satyricon*," in *Transactions and Proceedings of the American Philological Association* 89 [1958], pages 14–24.)

Phayllus. Greek stade racer/pentathlete, early 5th century, Croton. Phayllus won three victories in the Pythian games: two in the pentathlon and one in the stade. He also equipped and commanded the only Crotoniate ship of the Greek fleet which defeated the Persians at Salamis (480).

An epigram concerning Phayllus records that he long-jumped 55 feet and threw the discus 95 feet. While the latter distance seems probable enough, the former stretches credibility. Not surprisingly, it has evoked a good deal of comment from modern scholars. The consensus: either the Greek long jump was tripartite, perhaps a hop, skip and jump, or else the epigram is pure fiction.

Sources: Aristophanes *Acharnians* 215; *Wasps* 1206; Herodotus 8.47; *IAG* 11; Pausanias 10.9.2; Zenobius 6.23, the source of the epigram.

Pherenice. Greek trainer. *See* Pisirodus.

Pherias. Greek wrestler (boys'), 5th century, Aegina. Pherias attempted to enter the boys' wrestling at the 78th Olympiad (468), but was declared ineligible due to his extreme youth. He bided his time, returned in 464, gained official approval to wrestle, and won the event. Source: Pausanias 6.14.1.

Phidippides. Greek long distance runner, late 6th/early 5th century, Athens. Phidippides' moment of glory came not in the stadium, but as a result of his run from Athens to Sparta. The year was 490; the Persians were bearing down on Attica. The Athenians, not wishing to face the full force of the Persian army alone, sent an appeal to Sparta for help. Their message was delivered by Phidippides, who, according to Herodotus, arrived in Sparta the day after he left Athens. (He thus covered the distance between the two famous polises — 150 miles — in two days.)

Although the Spartans refused the Athenian request, Athens nonetheless prevailed against the Persians, at the Battle of Marathon. According to legend, a messenger ran the 26 miles from Marathon to Athens to announce the victory. For reasons that are not entirely clear, Phidippides has been popularly associated with this first "Marathon run," but it was not he; the runner's name is given in Plutarch as Eucles (q.v.). Source: Herodotus 6.105. Pliny the Elder (7.84) also records Phidippides' feat, but states that even Phidippides was surpassed by the Spartan Anystis and Alexander the

Great's messenger Philonides, both of whom ran the 148 miles from Sicyon to Elis in *one* day. The biographer Cornelius Nepos (*Lives* 1.4 [Miltiades]) also mentions Phidippides — he spells the name Phidippus — and refers to him as a *hemerodromus,* "day runner," a man who could run vast distances in one day.

Phidolas. Greek horse racer, 6th century, Corinth. Phidolas turned embarrassment into Olympic glory with the help of his horse, Aura. At the beginning of his race, Phidolas fell from his mount, but she continued the race without him, executing all the maneuvers properly, and crossing the finish line first. The judges proclaimed Phidolas the winner despite his failure to remain seated on Aura's back.

Phidolas' sons were also champion horse racers, although the number of their Olympic triumphs is disputed. Some accounts credit them with two wins, but the official records kept at Olympia state that their horse won only at the 68th Olympiad (508). SOURCES: *Greek Anthology* (attributed to Anacreon) 6.135; Pausanias 6.13.9–10. (For similar accounts of driverless horses winning races, *see* Corax.)

Philammon. Greek boxer. *See* Glaucus.

Philinus. Greek stade racer, 3rd century, Cos. Philinus was a highly successful runner, having won five Olympic crowns, four each at the Pythian and Nemean games, and an astounding eleven at the Isthmian games. SOURCES: Eusebius 207; Pausanias 6.17.2; Theocritus 2.115, and possibly 7.105, although there is some doubt about whether the Philinus mentioned here is the athlete.

Philippus. Greek event unknown, 6th century, Croton. Philippus, called by Herodotus the "best looking man of his day," had the good fortune to win an Olympic championship, and the bad fortune to fall in love with a woman from Sybaris at a time when the Sybarites and Croton were at war. Their planned marriage never took place; Philippus subsequently departed for Sicily, where he was killed in battle. SOURCE: Herodotus 5.47.

Philombrotus. Greek pentathlete, 7th century, Sparta. Philombrotus won three Olympic pentathlon championships, the first one coming in 676. (Moretti considers it likely that his second and third championships came in the following two Olympiads, 672 and 668.) SOURCE: Eusebius 197.

Philonides. Greek long distance runner. *See* Phidippides.

Philostratus. Greek heavy eventer. *See* Straton.

Philotus. Greek boxer (boys'), late 7th century, Sybaris. Philotus won the boys' boxing in 616, the first year in which it was an Olympic event. SOURCE: Eusebius 199; Pausanias 5.8.9, where the name is spelled Philytus; Philostratus 13.

Phlegyas. Greek pentathlete, dates and place of origin unknown, Pisa. Phlegyas may have been the best discus thrower in Olympic history. It is said that he practiced by hurling discuses across the Alpheus River, and that he always sent them on the fly to the opposite bank, a distance, according to Drees, of at least 150 feet. SOURCE: Statius 6.668ff. Statius provides a vivid account of the preparation to throw: "he roughens the discus and his hand with dirt, and then, after shaking off the dust, he turns it over in his hands to see which side fits better in his fingers, which side better in the crook of his arm."

Phormio. Greek boxer. *See* Eupolus.

Phylacidas. Greek pankratiast, 5th century, Aegina. Phylacidas won twice at the Isthmian games, once at the Nemean. He learned how to box from his fellow citizen Pytheas (q.v.), the subject of Pindar's *Nemean 5*. SOURCE: Pindar *Isthmian 6*.

Pisidorus. *See* Pisirodus.

Pisirodus (spelled Pisidorus in Philostratus). Greek boxer, 5th century, Rhodes. A boxing winner, Pisirodus continued the Rhodian tradition of athletic excellence begun by his grandfather, Diagoras (q.v.). An interesting story is told about his mother and trainer, Pherenice (the daughter of Diagoras). Wishing to accompany her son to his bouts, she disguised herself as a man. (Women were prohibited from viewing the competitions.) Unfortunately, her deception was discovered; the authorities, after some discussion, pardoned her in deference to her father. However, they also enacted a regulation requiring trainers as well as athletes to disrobe at future Olympiads. SOURCES: Pausanias 5.6.7–8; Philostratus 17.

Polites. Greek stade/diaulos/dolichos racer, 1st century A.D., Ceramus. Polites was *triastes* in the 212th Olympiad (A.D. 72). When discussing Polites, Pausanias adds the incidental information that the field for the stade race was narrowed by a series of heats, with the winner of each heat advancing to the finals. SOURCE: Eusebius 215; Pausanias 6.13.3–4.

Polycles (given the epithet *Polychalcus,* "much brazen"). Greek chariot racer, [5th century], Sparta. Polycles won a quadrigarian victory at Olympia, and also gained charioteering triumphs at the Pythian, Isthmian and Nemean games, thus earning him the title *periodonikes.* A statue group dedicated to him showed his two children beside him; one held a wheel, and the other was trying to snatch away his father's victory ribbon. SOURCE: Pausanias 6.1.7.

Polyctor. Greek wrestler, late 1st century, Elis. Polyctor advanced to the wrestling finals of the Olympics in 12 B.C., where he was to face Sosander of Smyrna for the championship. So intent was Polyctor's father, Damoniscus, that his son should win that he bribed Sosander's father to arrange for Sosander to throw the bout. Sosander apparently agreed to the deal, but the plot was exposed prior to the match. The judges imposed heavy fines on both fathers; they used the proceeds to construct statues. SOURCE: Pausanias 5.21.16.

Polydamas. (Sometimes spelled Pulydamas.) Greek pankratiast, late 5th century, Scotussa. Supposedly the tallest man on record, Polydamas won an unspecified number of pankration championships, including one at Olympia in 408. But like Milo of Croton (q.v.), his off-the-field exploits brought him a degree of fame equalling that which he earned as an athlete.

Several stories which defy credibility are told about this famous pankratiast. For example, he once killed a lion barehanded in an effort to rival Heracles' slaying of the Nemean Lion. On another occasion, he wandered into a herd of cattle and grabbed the largest bull by a hind hoof. He held fast as the bull struggled to escape, until finally the animal literally tore free, leaving only its hoof in Polydamas' grasp. On still another occasion, he stopped a fast-moving chariot by grabbing onto the back of the rig while simultaneously digging his heels into the ground until the chariot came to a halt.

So far had his fame spread that he was invited to Persia to meet the king. While there, he challenged three of the king's best soldiers — the Immortals — to a one-against-three fight, and defeated them all. (Portions of the marble relief illustrating Polydamas' exploits in Persia have been preserved.)

He died one hot summer afternoon as he and some friends were enjoying themselves in the shady coolness of a cave. When the roof of the cave suddenly began to give way, Polydamas attempted to prevent its collapse by supporting the ceiling with his arms as his friends scrambled to safety. Whether an altruistic gesture or a hubristic display of strength, no one could say, for Polydamas was crushed by falling rubble. His statue at Olympia was said to be capable of healing the sick. SOURCES: Dio Chrysostom 78.20; Eusebius 203; Diodorus Siculus 9.15; Lucian *Essays in Portraiture Defended* 19; *Herodotus* 8; *How to Write History* 34, 35; *Parliament of the Gods* 12; Pausanias 6.5.1; 4–9; Philostratus 1, 22, 43; Plato *Republic* 338C, where Plato alludes to Polydamas' meat diet and the additional strength it afforded him.

Polymnestor. Greek stade racer (boys'), early 6th century, Miletus. Polymnestor won the boys' stade in the 46th Olympiad (596). His training regimen apparently included the chasing of rabbits in pastures. SOURCES: Eusebius 199; Philostratus 13, 43; Solinus 1.97.

Polynices. Greek stade racer (boys'), 7th century, Elis. In the first year for boys' stade competitions at Olympia (632), Polynices was the winner. SOURCES: Eusebius 199; Pausanias 5.8.9.

Pompeius Musclosus. Roman charioteer, prior to the 2nd century A.D., place of origin unknown. Musclosus won 3,559 races during his career. *See* Appuleius Diocles.

Pontius Epaphroditus. Roman charioteer. *See* Appuleius Diocles.

Praemisit et vicit. (Literal meaning: "he sent [his rivals] ahead and won.") A Roman chariot racing strategy; its precise application to the racetrack is unclear. It probably referred to a race in which the ultimately victorious driver deliberately fell behind at the outset, only to rely on a finishing surge to win. Such a strategy would offer at least two advantages: (1) It would enable the driver to observe multivehicular crashes on the track ahead, and maneuver around them; (2) it would enable the horses to conserve their energy in the early going.

Praxidamas. Greek boxer, 6th century, Aegina. Praxidamas, along with Rhexibius (q.v.) of Opuntia, was the first athlete to dedicate a statue of himself at Olympia. Praxidamas' boxing championship came in 544. SOURCE: Pausanias 6.18.7.

Praxidamas. Greek wrestler, 5th century, Aegina. In addition to an Olympic championship, Praxidamas earned five crowns at the Isthmian games, and three at the Nemean. According to Pindar, his relatives won more boxing crowns than any family in Greece. The victory by Praxidamas' son Alcimidas in boys' wrestling at Nemea was the 25th crown festival championship won by a member of this illustrious family of athletes. SOURCE: Pindar *Nemean 6*.

Priscus. Roman gladiator, 1st century A.D., place of origin unknown. Priscus, along with his opponent Verus, was the subject of a short poem by Martial. The poet states that the two were evenly matched, and that at the end of their bout, the emperor (Domitian) sent each a wooden sword *(rudis)*, the symbol of discharge from service as a gladiator. The result: two men fought; each was a winner. SOURCE: Martial *Concerning Spectacles* 29.

Probus. Roman gladiator *(murmillo)*, dates unknown, Germany. Probus lived to the age of 49. No statistical information appears pertaining to his gladiatorial career; however, in addition to his *murmillo* classification, he is also identified as a *contrarete* (literal meaning: against the *retiarius*). This may indicate that *murmillones* were customarily paired with *retiarii*. SOURCE: *AE* 1971 (179).

Prolusio. A mock Roman gladiatorial bout which preceded the more serious matches.

Promachus. Greek pankratiast, 4th century, Pellana. Promachus won three pankration championships at the Isthmian games, two at the Nemean games and one at Olympia, the latter allegedly a result of a steamy love note from his girlfriend; the letter in reality had been forged by his coach for use as a motivational tool.

His Olympic victory supposedly came at the expense at Polydamas (q.v.), but the people of Polydamas' home area quite naturally rejected this, citing as part of the argument a verse of poetry referring to "undefeated Polydamas."

The Pellanians erected two statues of Promachus, one at Olympia, and one in the gymnasium in Pellana.
SOURCES: Pausanias 6.8.6; 7.27.5–6; Philostratus 22.

Protophanes. Greek wrestler/pankratiast. *See* Straton.

Prytanis. Greek boxer. *See* Eupolus.

Ptoeodorus. *See* Xenophon.

Pulydamas. *See* Polydamas.

Purple faction. *See* Faction.

Purpurius. Roman gladiator *(retiarius)*. *See* Rapidus.

Pythagoras. Greek boxer, early 6th century, Samos. Pythagoras attempted to enter the boys' boxing competitions at the 48th Olympiad (588), but was adjudged to be over the age limit. So he entered the men's division, and won it.

According to Diogenes Laertius (quoting Erastosthenes quoting Favorinus), Pythagoras was the first man to box *entechnos,* "scientifically" (probably meaning that he introduced various combinations of moves, feints and similar strategies). He wore his hair long, and came to Olympia clad in a purple robe. SOURCES: Diogenes Laertius 8.47; Eusebius 199.

Pythagoras. Greek stade/hoplite (?) racer, 3rd century, Magnesia on the Maeander. Pythagoras competed in the Olympic games of 300 and 296, winning the stade in each Olympiad. He also numbered among his crowns two Pythian, five Isthmian, seven Nemean, and two additional Olympian. SOURCES: Eusebius 205; *Papyrus Oxyrhyncus* 20.2082. A fragmentary name (only the final *sigma* is extant) in *P. Oxy.* 20.2082 refers to a Magnesian victor in the hoplite race. Moretti suggests the strong possibility that the unknown hoplite racer was this same Pythagoras.

Pytheas. Greek pankratiast (boys'), early 5th century, Aegina. Pytheas earned a crown in the boys' pankration at the Nemean games. He had two uncles who were also noted athletes: Euthymenes, who triumphed twice at Nemea, and once at Megara, and Themistius, who won both the boxing and the pankration events at Epidaurus. SOURCE: Pindar *Nemean* 5; *Isthmian* 5, 6.

Pythian games. One of the four Greek crown festivals, the quadrennial Pythian games were held in Delphi, in honor of Apollo.

Unlike most athletic festivals, the Pythian games also featured musical competitions.

Rapidus. Roman gladiator *(retiarius)*, dates unknown, Aquileia. The inscription which commemorates Rapidus is badly damaged, resulting in frequent lacunae at key points. Nevertheless, several reasonable hypotheses about his interesting career can be put forth.

The name Rapidus (meaning "quick, agile") was probably an epithet; the gladiator's full or real name has been lost. If Rapidus was indeed an epithet, it would fit well with the primary skill required of a *retiarius:* quickness, in order to elude opponents that were invariably more heavily armed.

The inscription reveals that this Rapidus died after his sixth bout; the tantalizing words *dicina dec* follow. Suggested restorations for the phrase include *in medicina decessit*, "he died in surgery." If correct, this implies that wounded gladiators were not dispatched like injured pack horses, but rather, the physicians employed by the gladiatorial bureaucracy made every effort to save their lives.

SOURCE: *CIL* 3.12925. *(AE* 1960 [139] pertains to a Greek *retiarius* by the name of Purpurius; the final line of the inscription, while almost hopelessly corrupt, may be translated as "he died in surgery" if one accepts an emendation of *moadu* to *medi[cina].)*

Ratumenna. Roman charioteer. *See* Corax.

Red; Reds; Red faction. *See* Faction.

Remissus. (Literal meaning: "sent back.") A poorly understood technical term from Roman chariot racing, it probably referred to a race in which a winner could not be determined due to the closeness of the finish. In such cases, the chariots would be "sent back" to run an additional lap. Efforts to equate *remissus* with *revocatus* should be rejected. The technical terminology of the race track was precise; terms were not used loosely or interchangeably.

Retiarius. The most easily recognizable kind of gladiator, a *retiarius* carried a dagger, trident and net (hence, *retiarius*, a word literally meaning "netman"), went bareheaded into the arena, and was protected by almost no body armor.

Revocatus. (Literal meaning: "called back.") A technical term in Roman chariot racing, its precise application is unclear. It may refer to a race in which there was a false start, thus necessitating the recall of the chariots to the starting line. This term should not be equated to *remissus*.

Rhexibius. Greek pankratiast, 6th century, Opus. Rhexibius, and Praxidamas (q.v.) of Aegina, were the first two athletes to dedicate statues of themselves at Olympia; Rhexibius' pankration victory occurred in 536. Source: Pausanias 6.18.7.

Rhipsolaus. Greek stade racer. *See* Olyntheus.

Rudiarii. *See* Rudis.

Rudis. (Literal meaning: "stirring stick," used in cooking.) A rudis was a wooden sword presented to a Roman gladiator upon his retirement. Hence, gladiators no longer active were called *rudiarii*.

Samnite (gladiator). *See* Secutor.

Samus. Roman gladiator *(murmillo/eques)*, 1st century A.D., place of origin unknown. The inscription pertaining to Samus was found on his house in Pompeii. Its unusual feature is that it identifies Samus as both a *murmillo* and an *eques*. It was highly irregular for gladiators to change classifications, or to fight in more than one classification. (*See also* Special Essay 2, pages 103–105.) Source: *CIL* 4.4420. Samus is also mentioned in 4340, 4377 and 4395.

Sarapion. Greek boxer (boys'), 1st century A.D., Alexandria. When Sarapion arrived in Olympia to compete in the games of A.D. 88, the local residents were suffering from a famine. He supplied them with food, and then went on to win a boxing championship. For these deeds, the Eleans dedicated a statue of Sarapion in one of their gymnasia. Source: Pausanias 6.23.6.

Sarapion. Greek pankratiast, 1st century A.D., Alexandria. At the 201st Olympiad (A.D. 25), Sarapion was so frightened of his pankration opponents that he fled the games. This act of cowardice was apparently unprecedented in the history of pankration competition at the Olympics. Source: Pausanias 5.21.18.

Satur. Roman gladiator *(murmillo)*. *See* Bassus.

Satyrus. Greek boxer, dates unknown, Elis. Satyrus triumphed five times in the Nemean games, and twice each at the Pythian and Olympic games. SOURCE: Pausanias 6.4.5.

Scirtus. Roman charioteer, 1st century A.D., place of origin unknown. A White faction driver, Scirtus raced chariots for twelve years, A.D. 13–25. His seasonal performances may be itemized as follows:

Year	Firsts	Firsts Revocatus	Seconds	Thirds
13	1	0	1	1
14	1	0	1	2
15	1	0	2	5
16	2	1	5	5
17	2	1	8	6
18	0	0	7	12
19	0	1	5	5
20	0	0	3	4
21	0	0	2	5
22	0	0	3	4
23	0	1	1	5
24	0	0	1	4
25	0	0	0	2
Totals	7	4	39	60

(Presumably, the four *revocatus* races were victories, not seconds or thirds.)

This inscription is particularly interesting because of its unique year-by-year itemization of Scirtus' statistics. Clearly, Scirtus' career follows the typical bell-shaped curve characteristic of most professional athletes throughout history: his best years were obviously A.D. 16–19, preceded by a gradual increase in proficiency (A.D. 13–15), and followed by a gradual decline (A.D. 20–25), with this statistics of his final year nearly matching the numbers he put up in his first year. SOURCE: *CIL* 6.10051.

Secular games. A theoretically centennial Roman festival held at the closing of a *saeculum* ("generation"). In actual practice, however, emperors sometimes decreed celebrations of the Secular games without regard to the 100-year requirement.

Secundus. Roman gladiator *(paegniarius)*, dates and place of origin unknown. Secundus lived to the advanced age of 99 years, nine months and 18 days. His longevity is perhaps to be explained in part by the fact that, as a *paegniarius*, he never competed with lethal weaponry. The curious words *in culice*, "in a mosquito," appear, evidently as a gloss, between the second and third lines of the inscription pertaining to Secundus. The precise application of this phrase is unclear, although it may refer to some mosquito-like characteristic of Secundus, perhaps light and darting. Secundus' epitaph concludes with the information that the whole *familia* of the Ludus Magnus erected his monument. SOURCE: *CIL* 6.10168.

Secutor. (Literal meaning: "pursuer"; sometimes called *Samnite*.) A kind of Roman gladiator equipped with a crested helmet, chest armor, and protective covering for the left leg. He carried a large shield and a sword. The heavily armed *secutor* was often matched with the much more lightly attired *retiarius*, whom he pursued about the arena floor.

Sergius. Roman gladiator, late 1st or early 2nd century A.D., place of origin unknown. The satirist Juvenal reserved some of his most acerbic language for a senator's wife, Eppia, who left her husband to run off with Sergius. Nor did Sergius escape the satirist's vituperative barbs; Juvenal mockingly describes the gladiator's cut arm, deformed and scarred face, the huge lump on his nose, a constantly watering eye. Eppia preferred this, according to Juvenal, to children and country, sister and husband.

Although the satirist does not indicate Sergius' classification, he evidently fought as a heavily armed gladiator, perhaps a Thracian or a Samnite. Juvenal does state that the lump on his nose resulted from the continual rubbing of his helmet. (Compare the visages of today's professional football players, especially linemen, for similar signs of helmet-induced abrasions.)

One final taunt may be inferred from Juvenal's use of the diminutive suffix *-olus*, which he applies to Sergius' name: Sergiolus. This may refer to nothing more than Sergius' physique or age, but given Juvenal's mindset, it is probably meant to convey a pejorative implication about the gladiator's societal status, especially when compared to the respectable position of Eppia's husband. SOURCE: Juvenal 6.82–113.

Sesterce. (Pl. **sesterces.**) Along with asses and denarii, a basic unit of Roman currency. The Edict of Diocletian (an early 4th century A.D. wage-prize freeze) specified maximum daily wages ranging from 80 to 200 sesterces for most workers.

Sica. *See* Thracian.

Singles race. A kind of Roman chariot race in which each driver competed for himself (as opposed to cooperating with one or more teammates). *See also* doubles race; triples race.

Sisinnes. Roman gladiator, dates unknown, Scythia. Lucian recounts the tale of Sisinnes and his friend Toxaris, who attended a gladiatorial show together. A particularly tall combatant was led into the arena by a herald, who announced to the crowd that the tall young man would fight any spectator, for a reward of 10,000 drachmas (for the volunteer). Perhaps in a moment of reckless bravado, Sisinnes took up the challenge. After entrusting his 10,000 drachmas (paid in advance) to Toxaris, he donned the armor, save for a helmet, and advanced bareheaded toward his opponent. Sisinnes suffered the first blow, a deep cut on the thigh, which bled profusely. His opponent, now overconfident, moved to dispatch Sisinnes, but the latter managed to summon enough strength to administer a fatal stab wound to the other man's chest. Sisinnes would also have died from his injury but for the swift intervention of Toxaris, who took him home and nursed him back to health.

After a long period of convalescence, Sisinnes recovered and subsequently married Toxaris' sister. But his leg remained lame for life. SOURCE: Lucian *Toxaris* 59–60.

Sosander. Greek wrestler. *See* Polyctor.

Sostratus. Greek pankratiast, 4th century, Sicyon. Sostratus gained the crown of victory in the pankration a combined 12 times at the Nemean and Isthmian games, three times at the Olympic games and twice at the Pythian games. He developed an innovative method of winning his matches: he gripped his opponent's fingers and bent them back until the pain became so intense that the opponent was compelled to yield. This enabled him to win all his matches *amachos*, "without a fight"; additionally, he acquired the epithet Acrochersites, "finger-tipper." SOURCES: *IAG* 25; Pausanias 6.4.1–3.

Sotades. Greek dolichos racer, early 4th century, Crete. Sotades won the dolichos at the Olympic games of 384. But in the next Olympiad, he represented Ephesus, having been bribed to do so by the Ephesians. His fellow citizens in Crete banished him for this act of disloyalty. SOURCE: Pausanias 6.18.6.

Spiculus. Roman gladiator *(murmillo)*, 1st century A.D., place of origin unknown. Apparently a favorite of Nero, Spiculus benefitted from his association with the emperor by munificent grants of a patrimony and a house. Near the end of Nero's reign, when he realized that a military coup against him was about to succeed, he called in vain for Spiculus to serve as his executioner. SOURCE: Suetonius *Life of Nero* 30; 47. The name Spiculus also appears in a Pompeian gladiatorial inscription (*CIL* 4.1474), and on a gladiatorial cup (*CIL* 12.5696, 32). Whether these two Spiculi are to be identified with Suetonius' Spiculus is conjectural.

Spina. The long dividing wall in the center of Roman chariot racetracks; seven circuits around the *spina* generally constituted one race. (According to Humphrey *[Roman Circuses]*, the standard word in ancient times for this wall was *euripus*.)

Stade race. A straight Greek foot race covering approximately 200 yards.

Stadion (Latinized form: **stadium**). Originally a measure of distance (about 200 yards), the word eventually was applied to the foot race of that distance, and ultimately to the facilities built to accommodate spectators of the Greek stade race.

Stomius. Greek pentathlete, 4th century, Elis. Stomius won a pentathlon championship at the Olympic games and three at the Nemean. The inscription on his victory statue at Olympia stated that as a solider in the Elean army, he killed an opposing general in single combat during a war against Sicyon. SOURCES: Diodorus Siculus 15.69; Pausanias 6.3.2.

Straton. Greek wrestler/pankratiast, 1st century, Alexandria. Straton won victories in the pankration and wrestling at the 178th Olympiad (68 B.C.). Two of his (potential?) opponents, Eudelus and Philostratus, were respectively convicted of receiving and offering bribes. They were thus evidently disqualified before Straton faced them, although Pausanias is not clear on this point.

A portico was constructed expressly for Straton's use in training in the city of Aegium.

SOURCES: Aelian *Various Histories* 4.15; Pausanias 5.21.8–10, where Pausanias lists the other athletes known to have won the pankration and wrestling at the same Olympiad: Caprus (q.v.) of Elis, Aristomenes of Rhodes and Protophanes of Magnesia on the Lethaeus, all prior to Straton; and after him, Marion of Alexandria, Aristeas of Stratoniceus and Nicostratus of Cilicia.

Stratophon. Greek boxer, dates and place of origin unknown. Like Apollophanes (q.v.) and Olympicus (q.v.), Stratophon's appearance had been greatly altered by the blows he suffered in boxing. Lucillius noted that Odysseus' dog Argos recognized him after a 20-year absence, but after four hours of boxing, no one, including the town dogs, could recognize Stratophon. SOURCE: *Greek Anthology* (Lucillius) 11.77.

Subpositicius. A term from the gladiatorial establishment. It should mean "substitute," but its exact application to Roman gladiatorial fighting is unclear. It probably referred to a gladiator who replaced a colleague unable to perform due to illness or injury.

Successit et vicit. (Literal meaning: "he came from behind and won.") A Roman chariot racing strategy; it apparently referred to a race in which the driver held back in the early going, but then came back to claim the victory at the finish.

Symmachus. *See* Damiscus.

Talent. A measure of money equalling 6,000 Greek drachmas. Its value can be gauged by considering that the average daily salary of a 5th century Greek worker may have been one drachma.

Taurosthenes. Greek wrestler, 5th century, Aegina. Taurosthenes, wrestling winner at the 84th Olympiad (444), devised an innovative method of informing his father (who had remained in Aegina) of his victory: He tied a red ribbon to the leg of a homing pigeon and released the bird. It flew straight to Aegina on the same day (a distance of about 100 miles), thus successfully conveying to

Taurosthenes' father the good news about his wrestling championship.

Pausanias relates that a phantom resembling Taurosthenes also appeared in Aegina to announce his victory; *see* Chimon. Sources: Aelian *Various Histories* 9.2; Pausanias 6.9.3. Pliny the Elder (10.71) recounts a story about a certain Caecina, owner of a quadriga in Volterra (near Rome), who would catch swallows, take them with him to the chariot races in Rome, and then paint the color of the winning faction(s) on their legs before releasing them. The birds returned immediately to Volterra, thus incidentally informing Caecina's friends which factions had won.

Tetraites. Roman gladiator. *See* Petraites.

Thaeaus. Greek wrestler, 5th century, Argos. Thaeaus twice triumphed in wrestling at Argos, in addition to three victories at the Isthmian games, and one each at the Pythian and Nemean. He also claimed wins at festivals in Sicyon and Athens.

His relatives Thrasyclus and Antias were also prizewinning athletes. According to Pindar, they won so many bronzes there would not be time to count them. Source: Pindar *Nemean* 10.

Theagenes. (Sometimes spelled Theogenes.) Greek boxer/pankratiast/dolichos racer, flourished 480–460, Thasos. Theagenes' strength first drew attention when, at the age of nine, he carried home a large bronze statue from the town square. An epigram on Theagenes, quoted by Athenaeus, illustrates his prodigious appetite: "And on a wager I once ate a Maeonian ox; for my own country Thasos could not have furnished a meal to Theagenes; whatever I ate, I kept asking for more. For this reason I stand in bronze, holding forth my hand." (10.412E.) (Loeb Classical Library translation.)

Theagenes won an Olympic boxing and pankration championship, and three more in boxing at the Pythian games. He also competed successfully at the Nemean games (nine championships), and at the Isthmian games (ten championships); in each case, he gained some of the crowns in boxing, some in the pankration. His career victory total, including wins at the smaller and presumably less competitive local festivals, was either 1,400 (Pausanias), or 1,200 (Plutarch, who considered most of his 1,200 crowns meaningless, having been won against inferior or nonexistent competition).

At the 75th Olympiad (480), he entered both the boxing and pankration contests, defeating Euthymus (q.v.) in the former. However, he was so drained from boxing that he could not summon the strength to compete in the pankration, thereby incurring a fine from the judges.

After he died, one of his enemies approached his statue on a nightly basis and flogged it, a misdeed which the perpetrator would scarcely have dared to commit while Theagenes lived. At last, after one such flogging, the statue crashed down upon the miscreant and killed him. The citizens of Thasos, judging the statue guilty of murder, removed it and sank it far out at sea, an act which brought down upon them the wrath of the gods in the form of a famine. The famine did not abate until the Thasians retrieved the statue and restored it to its place of honor, where it was said to have curative powers. SOURCES: Athenaeus 10.412 D, E, F; Dio Chrysostom 31.95–97; *IAG* 21; Lucian *Parliament of the Gods* 12; Pausanias 6.6.5–6; 6.11.2–9; 6.15.3; Plutarch *Moral Essays* 811D, E. (Plutarch held Theagenes in low esteem, calling him an arrogant and contentious glory-seeker.)

Theantus. Greek boxer. *See* Alcaenetus.

Themistius. Greek boxer/pankratiast. *See* Pytheas.

Theochrestus. Greek chariot racer, [4th century], Cyrene. Theochrestus, and his father and grandfather, were noted horse breeders. He and his grandfather each won Olympic chariot race victories, while his father earned a crown at the Isthmian games. SOURCE: Pausanias 6.12.7.

Theogenes. *See* Theagenes.

Theognetus. Greek wrestler (boys'), dates unknown, Aegina. That Theognetus won a boys' wrestling championship at Olympia did not capture Pausanias' attention as much as the fact that Theognetus' victory statue depicted him holding a pine cone and a pomegranate. SOURCES: Pausanias 6.9.1; Pindar *Pythian 8*. A certain Theognetus, also a wrestler, appears in a short epigram in the *Greek Anthology* (Simonides) 16.2. He may be the same athlete mentioned by Pausanias and Pindar.

Theopompus, Greek pentathlete; and **Theopompus,** Greek wrestler. *See* Damaretus.

Thessalus. This Greek event is uncertain. *See* Xenophon.

Thracian. A kind of Roman gladiator equipped with a visored helmet, full length arm wrappings, a small shield (either round or square), waist-to-knee leg wrappings and knee-to-foot shin guards. A Thracian gladiator also brandished a short, curved sword called a *sica.*

Thrasybalus. Greek chariot racer. *See* Xenocrates.

Thrasyclus. Greek wrestler(?). *See* Thaeaus.

Timanthes. Greek pankratiast, dates unknown, Cleonae. After Timanthes won his Olympic pankration championship, he retired from active competition, but stayed fit by bending and shooting a large bow. On one occasion, his bow-shooting routine was disrupted by a trip away from his home. Upon his return, he found himself unable to handle the bow, an eventuality which so depressed him that he committed suicide by self-immolation. SOURCE: Pausanias 6.8.4.

Timasitheus. Greek wrestler, 6th century, Croton. Timasitheus broke the Olympic wrestling victory string of his famous fellow-townsman, Milo (q.v.), at six. He employed a tactic of avoidance, apparently inducing Milo to engage in chasing him, thus fatiguing the older man. (Compare the similar strategy used centuries later by the boxer Melancomas [q.v.].) SOURCE: Pausanias 6.14.5.

Timasitheus. Greek pankratiast, 6th century (died 510), Delphi. Timasitheus won two pankration crowns in the Olympic games, and three in the Pythian. He was also a soldier of bravery and daring, but his luck ran out when he cast his lot with Isagoras of Athens during the latter's ill-fated attempt to capture the Acropolis. Timasitheus was taken prisoner and executed. SOURCES: Herodotus 5.72, who says that he could, if he wished, relate great stories about Timasitheus' prowess. Unfortunately, he chose not to do so. Pausanias 6.8.6.

Timodemus. *See* Four brother athletes.

Timodemus of Acharnae. Greek pankratiast, early 5th century, Acharnae. Timodemus won pankration championships at the Olympic Isthmian and Nemean games. His sons (also presumably heavy eventers) gained a total of four Pythian triumphs, eight Isthmian and seven Nemean. SOURCE: Pindar *Nemean 2*.

Timon. Greek pentathlete, [early 2nd century], Elis. Timon won championships in the pentathlon at all the crown festivals except the Isthmian, where the Eleans customarily refused to compete. SOURCE: Pausanias 5.2.1–4; 6.16.2. In 5.2.1–4, Pausanias offers three explanations for the Elean boycott; the most likely, in his view, could be traced to the time of Heracles, when several Elean ambassadors were murdered by the Argives. Elis' response to this outrage was to press Corinth to bar Argive athletes from the Isthmian games; when the Corinthians refused to do so, the Eleans instituted their boycott.

Tisamenus. Greek pentathlete, 5th century, Elis. Tisamenus became an Olympic athlete more by chance than by design. He had traveled to Delphi to inquire of Apollo's oracle the reason for his childless marriage. In the course of her reply, the Pythian priestess informed him that he was destined to win five great contests. Although the five great contests pertained to military actions, Tisamenus understood the phrase to refer to the pentathlon. So he went into training, journeyed to Olympia to compete, and came within a single contest of winning the event. Tisamenus triumphed in the long jump and the foot race; his opponent Hieronymus of Andros took the javelin and the discus. The overall outcome was apparently decided when Hieronymus prevailed in wrestling.

Tisamenus later served as a soothsayer for the Greek army at the Battle of Plataea (479).

SOURCES: Herodotus 9.33; Pausanias 3.11.6; 6.14.13.

Tisander. Greek boxer, flourished 540–524, Naxos (in Sicily, not the Cycladic island). Tisander won four Olympic boxing championships, four Pythian championships, and unrecorded numbers of crowns at the Nemean and Isthmian games. His training regimen included long swims around the promontories near his home, an exercise which he believed strengthened his arms to the degree necessary for success in his event. SOURCES: Pausanias 6.13.8; Philostratus 43.

Triastes. An honorary title applied to a Greek athlete who had won three foot races (probably the stade, diaulos and either the hoplite race or the dolichos) at the same festival.

Trigae. A kind of Roman racing chariot drawn by three horses.

Triples race. A kind of Roman chariot race in which three drivers from the same faction cooperated with each other to try to gain victory for one of them. *See also* singles race; doubles race.

Tritanus. Roman gladiator (Samnite), probably 1st century A.D., place of origin unknown. Pliny the Elder refers to Tritanus as a highly skilled gladiator who, despite his small frame, possessed exceptional strength. SOURCE: Pliny the Elder 7.81.

Troilus. Greek chariot racer, 4th century, Elis. Troilus competed in the 102nd Olympiad (372), the same year in which he served as an umpire. He won two chariot races that year (one using full-grown horses, the other with foals). His victories may have been somehow tainted, for the authorities subsequently passed a law prohibiting umpires from competing in the charioteering competitions. SOURCES: *IAG* 19; Pausanias 6.1.4–5.

Tryphosa. Greek stade racer, mid–1st century A.D., Tralles Caesarea. Tryphosa, sister of Hedea (q.v.) and Dionysia (q.v.), won championships at the Pythian and Isthmian games. SOURCE: *IAG* 63.

Marcus Ulpius Felix. Roman gladiator *(murmillo)*, dates unknown, Tunger. Marcus Ulpius Felix lived to the age of 45, but there is no indication of the number of bouts or victories. The last half of the stone is devoted to the names of those who made the monument: his wife, Syntache, and son, Iustus. SOURCE: *CIL* 6.10177.

Veianius. Roman gladiator, 1st century B.C., place of origin unknown. The poet Horace refers briefly to Veianius, as a gladiator who, upon retiring from the arena, placed his gladiatorial equipment in a shrine of Hercules, thus rendering it inaccessible when his admirers tried to persuade him to return to active service. SOURCE: Horace *Epistles* 1.1.4–6.

Vela. Many amphitheaters in the Roman world were equipped with *vela*, awnings or canopies which could be unfurled to cover the seating areas in the event of inclement weather.

Venatio. A Roman wild beast hunt, one of the kinds of entertainment sometimes featured in the amphitheaters.

Verus. Roman gladiator. *See* Priscus.

Vitalis. Roman gladiator *(retiarius)*, dates unknown, Batavia. Vitalis is called *invictus* ("unconquered") in the inscription providing his biographical data. However, the text also implies that Vitalis died in his final bout "together with his opponent," suggesting that they succumbed simultaneously to wounds which they had inflicted upon one another. Vitalis' epithet *invictus* makes this unlikely, although if both men died, the match would have been a draw, not a defeat. Therefore, *invictus* would have been technically accurate, albeit somewhat vainglorious. SOURCE: *CIL* 11.1070.

White; Whites; White faction. *See* Faction.

Wrestling. A Greek event in which the athlete stood facing his opponent, and then, through a series of holds, moves and feints, attempted to cause his opponent to fall backwards onto the ground. Pinning was unnecessary. Winning two of three such falls was required for victory in this event.

Xenarces. Greek pankratiast, 5th century(?), Stratus. Xenarces was the first man from Stratus to win an Olympic crown in the pankration. He also won an unspecified number of championships at the Pythian and Isthmian games, and at Argos. SOURCE: Pausanias 6.2.1–2.

Xenocrates. Greek chariot racer, early 5th century, Acragas. Xenocrates was awarded charioteering crowns in the Isthmian games, the Pythian games (of 490) and also in Athens. Nicomachus was his charioteer at the latter two, whereas his son Thrasybalus drove his chariot to victory in the Isthmian games. SOURCES: Pindar *Pythian* 6; *Isthmian* 2; Scholiast on Pindar *Pythian* 1.

Xenophon. Greek stade/diaulos racer pentathlete, flourished 470–460, Corinth. Before departing for Olympia in 464, Xenophon vowed to the goddess Aphrodite that if he won there, he would recruit fifty courtesans to serve in her shrine. The goddess must have assented, for Xenophon won a total of three Olympic championships, including crowns in both the stade and the pentathlon in the games of 464. According to Pindar, his double victory in these two events was unprecedented in Olympic history.

He won twice at the Isthmian games and an unspecified number of times at the Nemean games. He triumphed six times at the Pythian games, including another unique double victory, this time in the stade and the diaulos. He also won championships in festivals held in Athens, Corinth, Argos and Arcadia.

His grandfather Ptoeodorus, his father Thessalus, and several other relatives were also noted athletes.

SOURCES: Athenaeus 13.573E, F; Diodorus Siculus 11.70; Dionysius of Halicarnassus 9.61; Eusebius 203; Pausanias 4.24.5; Pindar *Olympian 13*.

Young men's division; Youths' division. *See* Men's division.

IV. Special Essays

1. *The Strange Case of Melissus of Thebes*

Pindar's third and fourth *Isthmian* odes are devoted to a Theban athlete named Melissus. In *Isthmian* 3, he is identified as a chariot race winner; in 4, as a pankratiast — a curiosity which, surprisingly, has failed to attract the attention of Pindaric scholars.

There are a good many examples of successful multi-event competitors presented elsewhere in this book, but the events were invariably those which demanded similar skills and physiques. Athletes who triumphed as boxers and pankratiasts were not uncommon; nor were stade/diaulos/dolichos winners. A charioteer/pankratiast combination, however, defies competitive reality. The likelihood that the same man could reasonably expect to taste victory or even credibly compete in these two events is unimaginably remote; the evidence pertaining to the ancient Greek athletic establishment will not admit of such an interpretation.

Let us consider some of that evidence, adduced within the pages of this book. Thirty-one different athletes (discounting Melissus) are honored by Pindaric epiniceans; none was a charioteer/pankratiast. The names of approximately 230 athletes appear in Books 5 and 6 of Pausanias; none of these 230 competed as a charioteer/pankratiast. The 4th century Lycaean victor list records the names of some 45 athletes; none was a charioteer/pankratiast. Several inscribed tablets found near Oropus preserve the names of about 78 athletes; none of the 78 was a charioteer/pankratiast. The Samian victor list from the 2nd century contains the names of nine athletes; all shunned the charioteering/pankration combination. A list of victorious athletes from the 121st Olympiad includes 13 names; no charioteer/pankratiasts appear. Photius' list commemorating the winners in the 177th Olympiad contains 15 names; none of these athletes was a charioteer/pankratiast.

From a sample of over 400 Greek athletes, from nearly every era and from disparate kinds of athletic festivals, there is not one who competed in the two events. In the face of this, can we plausibly assume that Melissus was the lone exception?

Hardly. If he were such a *rara avis*, Pindar surely would have said as much. After all, the poet fairly gushed over the achievement of Xenophon (*Ol.* 13) in winning both the stade and the pentathlon, two events that would logically complement each other. Can we assume that he would have no comment on what certainly would have been the only charioteering/pankration championship in crown festival history?

How, then, might the charioteer/pankratiast Melissus be explained? Several hypotheses emerge; the two most likely:

1. Pindar wrote two separate epiniceans for two different Theban athletes. Several champion athletes from the same town shared the same name. Examples: Isodorus the stade racer and Isodorus the horse racer, both from Thebes (*IG* 7.416); Metrodorus the dolichos racer and Metrodorus the pentathlete, both from Smyrna (*IG* 7.420); Sarapion the pankratiast (Pausanias 5.21.18) and Sarapion the stade racer (Eusebius 207). The first two pairs of athletes are differentiated by dissimilar patronymics; the third, by the different time periods in which they competed.

2. Melissus competed as a pankratiast, and was also a chariot owner, but not driver; such a situation was rare, but not unattested. A certain Sosibius (Callimachus *Fragment* 384) began his career as a dolichos racer/wrestler; after apparently watching his wealth increase and his athletic skills diminish, he eventually decided to retire from active competition and invest instead in chariots, with which he won crowns at the Nemean and Isthmian games. Melissus' career might have evolved similarly.

2. The Noteworthy Career of the Gladiator Hermes

The Roman epigrammatist and social critic Martial (d. A.D. 104) chose gladiators and charioteers as the subjects of several of his poems. The gladiator Hermes (5.24.), immortalized in Martialian verse, was probably a type rather than a specific individual. Martial's poem about him raises some interesting and occasionally abstruse points about the career of a Roman gladiator.

1   Hermes, hero of the Martian crowd,
2   Hermes, skilled in all the bouts allowed,
3   Hermes, who serves as gladiator and teacher,
4   Hermes, in his own school a fearsome creature,
5   Hermes, the only one Sunny-boy fears to fight,
6   Hermes, the only one that makes Flash white with fright,
7   Hermes, trained to win but not to club,
8   Hermes, the man himself is his own sub,
9   Hermes helps the ticket-scalpers pay their debts,
10 Hermes, the care and labor of the gladiatorettes,
11 Hermes, cocky with his warlike spear,
12 Hermes, with fishy trident has no peer,
13 Hermes, respected with drooping crest,
14 Hermes, of men of Mars the best,
15 Hermes, all these, three gladiators in one.

A number of useful details about a gladiator's career can be gleaned from this epigram.

In the second line, Martial states that Hermes was trained in all kinds of fighting, a rare instance of a gladiator plying his trade in more than one of the gladiatorial classifications. Other evidence overwhelmingly suggests that if a man began his career as (for example) a *retiarius*, he remained a *retiarius* until his death or retirement.

Martial indicates in the seventh line that Hermes was so proficient that he could force an opponent to yield without seriously injuring him.

Another example of Hermes' prowess appears in the following line, where Martial notes that he never required the services of a *subpositicius*. The word is a hapax legomenon in gladiatorial literature, and hence difficult to translate with confidence; "substitute" is perhaps the best rendering. However, the notion that a wounded or fatigued gladiator could call upon a substitute is highly implausible. A gladiatorial contest was a "one-on-one" affair, continuing until a conclusion was reached. Certainly, a practice as significant to the outcome as a substitution system would have received mention elsewhere in the sources. Perhaps a *subpositicius* was one who replaced a gladiator forced by illness or injury to withdraw prior to the announced day of a match. The indomitable Hermes never found himself incapacitated to the point where he failed to appear for a bout.

Efforts to equate *subpositicius* with the Greek *ephedros* are fanciful and should be discounted.

In line nine the word *locarius* (rendered as "ticket-scalper") appears. The precise meaning of *locarius* is uncertain; the root suggests that it referred to a person who was in some way connected with seats or seating arrangements in the amphitheater. The lexicographers Lewis and Short define it as "one who first took possession of a seat in the theatre and let it out to one who came later"; the *Oxford Latin Dictionary* states that a *locarius* is "one who buys up theatre seats as an investment." Hence, to suggest that a *locarius* was an ancient version of a ticket-scalper — that is, a speculator who, months in advance, acquires prime tickets to athletic events certain to attract large crowds, and then on the day of the event sells the tickets for far more than their face value — may not miss the mark too widely. A gladiatorial show featuring the famous Hermes would have been expected to fill the amphitheater; for this reason, Martial calls him *divitiae locariorum*, a source of riches for the ticket-scalpers.

In line ten, the reader is informed that Hermes was the object of concern and worry of the *ludiae*, variously rendered as female gladiator, wife of a gladiator, or mistress of a gladiator.

Martial indicates in line twelve that Hermes fought as a *retiarius*. The connection between the *retiarius'* equipment and the sea emerges in the phrase *aequoreo tridente*, "the sea's trident." Lines eleven and thirteen contain information about the other two classifications in which Hermes performed as a gladiator, but the overly general nature of the descriptions precludes successful attempts to determine which classifications.

The epigram concludes by noting Hermes' prowess and versatility in the three styles of fighting mentioned in lines eleven through thirteen: *ter unus*, three gladiators in one.

3. Athletic Dilettantes, Both Greek and Roman

Alcibiades. Chariot racer, 5th century B.C. (450–404), Athens. Alcibiades was a flamboyant and unpredictable Athenian orator and general. He assumed a major role in Athens during the Peloponnesian War (431–404), emerging as the prime proponent of an invasion of Sicily. His persuasive arguments in public debates on the propriety of the invasion led to his appointment as one of its leaders.

Shortly after setting sail for Sicily (in 415), Alcibiades was recalled to Athens to stand trial on a charge of desecrating a number of Herms (portrait busts of the gods) during one of his drunken rampages. Rather than face his accusers, he fled to Sparta, and then to Persia and Samos, before eventually returning to Athens and a triumphant homecoming in 407. His new popularity was short-lived, however, and he was murdered in Phrygia a few years later.

Alcibiades was famed for his horse breeding and for the number of racing chariots which he owned. In the chariot races of the Olympic games of 416, he entered a record seven chariots. According to the historian Thucydides, his drivers took the first, second and fourth places; the playwright Euripides asserts that the first, second and third places went to chariots entered by Alcibiades.

His duplicity is illustrated by a story told about one of his friends, Diomedes, who was very eager to win a chariot racing crown at Olympia. This Diomedes had heard that there was a fine racing chariot in the city of Argos; he prevailed upon Alcibiades — who was well-connected at Argos — to buy it for him. Alcibiades made the purchase, but kept the chariot for himself. Diomedes was furious, but when he complained, Alcibiades merely told him to do whatever he wished about the matter, which was presumably nothing. (For a full account of the life of Alcibiades, *see* the Plutarchian biography.)

Caligula. (Full name: Gaius Julius Caesar Germanicus; often referred to as Gaius), 1st century A.D. (12–41), Rome. Upon his accession to the emperorship in 37, Caligula sponsored a number of gladiatorial shows, which featured not only the standard matches, but also bouts between African and Campanian boxers. He expanded the program of chariot races in the Circus Maximus, so that they began early in the morning and continued to late at night. On some of the special race days, he decorated the Circus with green and red bunting, while men of senatorial rank drove the chariots. He commissioned games on the spur of the moment, as dictated by public demand. He also produced games and shows of various kinds in Sicily and Gaul.

Midway through his reign, he suddenly became excessively cruel; the cause of this unexpected change in his behavior has evoked a good deal of scholarly commentary and speculation, but whatever its genesis, it resulted in unprecedented troubles for the Roman people. At gladiatorial shows, it now became his occasional practice to withdraw the *vela* at the hottest time of the day, while simultaneously forbidding anyone to leave. He matched aged and worn out gladiators with wild beasts and required respectable but crippled or lame citizens to fight in the arena.

During one of his illnesses, a number of freeborn men vowed to fight as gladiators if he recovered. When he did indeed regain his health, he compelled them to fulfill their vows, forcing one man to fight at length until he was victorious, and finally releasing him only after many pleas on the gladiator's part.

He soon yearned to appear in the circus and the arena as an active participant. He donned the gear of the Thracians, and performed as a gladiator using genuine swords and shields. He demonstrated his partiality to the Thracians by reducing the amount of armor that could be worn by their opponents, the *murmillones.* He drove chariots in many places, and became particularly devoted to the Green faction, so much so that he often ate and slept in their stables.

His athletic career was cut short by a successful assassination attempt in 41. (See Suetonius' *Life of Caligula.)*

Commodus. (Full name: Lucius Aelius Aurelius Commodus), A.D. (161–192), Rome. Commodus, son and successor to Marcus Aurelius, the last of Rome's so-called "Five Good Emperors," did not continue his father's wise and moderate policies. He was only nineteen years of age when he became emperor, and the trappings and powers of the office soon went to his head. He vigorously persecuted the Roman Senate; he promoted his own (often incompetent) cronies to important advisory positions while ousting men of better judgment; he fancied himself to be the second coming of Hercules, sometimes dressing in a lion skin and wielding a club. And, like Nero before him, he longed to be the cynosure on the track and in the arena. As the historian Dio Cassius tells it (73.19, 22):

> . . . He descended to the arena from his place above and cut down all the domestic animals that approached him and some also that were led up to him or were brought before him in nets. He also killed a tiger, a hippopotamus, and an elephant. Having performed these exploits, he would retire, but later, after luncheon, would fight as a gladiator. The form of contest that he practised and the armour that he used were those of *secutores,* as they were called: he held the shield in his right hand and the wooden sword in his left, and indeed

took great pride in the fact that he was left-handed. His antagonist would be some athlete or perchance a gladiator armed with a wand; sometimes it was a man that he himself challenged, sometimes one chosen by the people, for in this as well as other matters he put himself on an equal footing with the other gladiators, except for the fact that they entered the lists for a very small sum, whereas Commodus received a million sesterces from the gladiatorial fund each day. Standing beside him as he fought were Aemilius Laetus, the prefect, and Eclectus. . . . When he had finished his sparring match, and of course won it, he would then, just as he was, kiss these companions through his helmet. After this the regular contestants would fight. The first day he personally paired all the combatants down in the arena, where he appeared with all the trappings of Mercury, including a gilded wand, and took his place on a gilded platform. . . . Later he would ascend to his customary place and from there view the remainder of the spectacle with us.

. . . He actually cut off the head of the Colossus, and substituted for it a likeness of his own head; then, having given it a club and placed a bronze lion at its feet, so as to cause it to look like Hercules, he inscribed on it, in addition to the list of his titles . . . these words: "Champion of *secutores*; only left-handed fighter to conquer twelve times (as I recall the number) one thousand men." (Loeb Classical Library translation.)

Nero. (Full name: Nero Claudius Caesar), 1st century A.D. (37–68), Rome. Nero ruled Rome as emperor from 54 to 68. A man with negligible native athletic ability, but a boundless supply of pretense, he seemed determined to etch his name into the annals of ancient sport history.

Early in his reign (59), he established the Juvenales, games which included chariot races, a gladiatorial show and stage plays. Old men and women of nobility were encouraged to participate. The chariot races featured quadrigae drawn by camels. Four hundred senators and 600 equestrians, Neronian draftees all, fought in the gladiatorial show.

Not long after, he founded a quinquennial festival called the Neronia; it consisted of competitions in music, gymnastics and horse racing. He also constructed a gymnasium, where he supplied members of the senatorial and equestrian classes with oil.

But Nero was not content with merely producing shows; he graced many of them with his active participation. From childhood, he had had a special affinity for chariot racing. Once, while discussing with his schoolmates a Green faction driver who had been thrown from his chariot and dragged behind it, his teacher overheard and reprimanded him. He deviously replied that he was referring to Hector (who had suffered a similar fate, as recorded by Homer in the *Iliad*). Nero owned a board game which utilized model chariots made of ivory; at the beginning of his reign, he played it constantly. He increased the number of races held in the Circus Maximus, so that the racing program extended until nightfall. Eventually, the desire to drive a chariot himself overcame him. He began by training and practicing in his private gardens, with slaves and idlers as his audience; later, he graduated to the Circus Maximus.

Encouraged by his performances in the Circus at Rome, he decided to grant to the organizers and judges of the Olympic games the honor of adding his name to the list of competitors there. He drove a ten-horse chariot, a deed which he himself had criticized others for doing. However, ten horses were evidently more than he could handle, for he lost control during the race and was thrown from the chariot. (The delightful phrase used by the biographer Suetonius, *excussus curru et rursus repositus*, "thrown from the chariot and put back again," clearly implies that the emperor could not regain his place in the rig under his own power; he required the assistance of bystanders.) Although he could not finish the race, he was nonetheless awarded the crown of victory.

After his glorious successes in Greece, he returned to Rome via Naples, where he was escorted through the city by a phalanx of white horses. When he had eventually made his way to the capital, he entered as part of a vast parade, in the same chariot which Augustus had used in similar triumphal processions. He was decked out in a purple robe and a star-studded cloak; footmen preceded him, bearing placards telling the stories of his athletic and musical victories at the crown festivals.

The world lost this great artist in 68, before he had time to accomplish several other athletic goals, including: (1) wrestling at Olympia. He practiced wrestling constantly and took a keen interest in viewing and judging wrestling matches during his travels in Greece. (2) Continuing his chariot racing career. He thought that he was the equal of the Sun in this activity. (3) Fighting a lion in the amphitheater. He had a specially trained lion that he had planned to kill in the arena by choking it, à la Hercules.

All these grandiose schemes were, unfortunately, cut short by his untimely death. *(See* Suetonius' *Life of Nero.)*

Spartacus. Gladiator, 1st century B.C., Thrace. Spartacus was a Thracian by birth; at one time he served in the Roman army, but later he was taken prisoner and sold to be trained as a gladiator. He was sent to Capua in 73 where he became a member of the gladiatorial school owned there by a certain Lentulus Batiatus. Spartacus and his fellow gladiators were evidently subject to constant mistreatment by their owner; they formed a plot to escape from Capua and return to their homes. Although about 200 men were in on the initial phase of the plan, they were betrayed. Only about 70 managed to escape, and they only by quick and decisive action. They overpowered their guards and seized clubs and swords from people on the streets. They also had the good fortune to encounter and take possession of some wagons carrying arms for gladiators at another school. Then, joined by other slaves and also by some freedmen, they established a position on Mt. Vesuvius. Spartacus was selected as the leader.

For the next several years, Spartacus and his renegade army (which may have numbered close to 90,000 men) defeated the forces sent against them by Rome. Finally, in 71, a Roman army under the command of Marcus Licinius Crassus cornered Spartacus and crushed the rebellion. Spartacus and most of his adherents were killed. *(See* Plutarch *Life of Crassus.)*

4. A Fifth Century A.D. Binarum *Chariot Race*

The fifth century poet Sidonius Apollinaris has left us a vividly worded description of a chariot race in which two teammates cooperated to ensure victory for one of them. The following poem is addressed to one of the charioteers, Consentius. Although the date of the poem places it outside the chronological limitations established for the Roman biographies, it has been included because it provides an excellent account of the transcendent rigors and excitement of the track, while also incidentally recounting the advantages of the *praemisit et vicit* strategy. (Sidonius Apollinaris *To Consentius* [23.317–427].)

> Thereupon, in the part where the door is and the seat of the consuls, round which there runs a wall with six vaulted chambers on each side, wherein are the starting-pens, you chose one of the four chariots by lot and mounted it, laying a tight grip on the hanging

reins. Your partner did the same; so did the opposing side. Brightly gleam the colors, white and blue, green and red, your several badges. Servants' hands hold mouth and reins and with knotted cords force the twisted manes to hide themselves, and all the while they incite the steeds, eagerly cheering them with encouraging pats and instilling a rapturous frenzy. There behind the barriers chafe those beasts, pressing against the fastenings, while a vapoury blast comes forth between the wooden bars, and even before the race, the field they have not yet entered is filled with their panting breath. They push, they bustle, they drag, they struggle, they rage, they jump, they fear and are feared; never are their feet still, but restlessly they lash the hardened timber. At last the herald with loud blare of trumpet calls forth the impatient teams and launches the fleet chariots into the field. The swoop of forked lightning, the arrow sped by Scythian string, the trail of the swiftly-falling star, the leaden hurricane of bullets whirled from Balearic slings has never so rapidly split the airy paths of the sky. The ground gives way under the wheels and the air is smirched with the dust that rises in their track. The drivers, while they wield the reins, ply the lash; now they stretch forward over the chariots with stooping breasts, and so they sweep along, striking the horses' withers and leaving their backs untouched. With charioteers so prone it would puzzle you to pronounce whether they were more supported by the pole or by the wheels. Now as if flying out of sight on wings, you had traversed the more open part, and you were hemmed in by the space that is cramped by craft, amid which the central barrier has extended its long, low double walled structure. [The *spina* is meant.] When the farther turning post freed you all from restraint once more, your partner went ahead of the two others, who had passed you; so then, according to the law of the circling course, you had to take the fourth track. [The other three drivers, having moved ahead of Consentius, now occupy the three inside lanes; he is relegated to the outside position.] The drivers in the middle were intent that if haply the first man, embarrassed by a dash of his steeds too much to the right, should leave a space open on the left by heading for the surrounding seats, he should be passed by a chariot driven in on the near side. As for you, bending double with the very force of the effort you keep a tight rein on your team and with consummate skill wisely reserve them for the seventh [and final] lap. [This illustrates one of the main advantages of the *praemisit* strategy: a team well rested for the final and perhaps decisive lap.] The others are busy with hand and voice, and everywhere the sweat of drivers and flying steeds falls in drops onto the field. The hoarse roar from applauding partisans stirs the heart, and the contestants, both horses and men, are warmed by the race and chilled by fear. Thus they go once round, then a second time; thus goes the third lap, thus the fourth; but in the fifth turn, the foremost man, unable to bear the pressure of his pursuers, swerved his car aside, for he had found, as he gave command to his fleet team, that their strength was exhausted. Now the return half of

the sixth course was completed and the crowd was already clamour-
ing for the award of the prizes; your adversaries, with no fear of any
effort from you, were scouring the track in front with never a care,
when suddenly you tautened the curbs all together, tautened your
chest, planted your feet firmly in front, and chafed the mouths of
your swift steeds.... Hereupon one of the others, clinging to the
shortest route round the turning post, was hustled by you, and his
team, carried away beyond control by their onward rush, could no
more be wheeled round in a harmonious course. As you saw him
pass before you in disorder, you got ahead of him by remaining
where you were, cunningly reining up. The other adversary, ex-
ulting in the public plaudits, ran too far to the right, close to the spectators; then as he turned aslant and all too late after long indifference
urged his horses with the whip, you sped straight past your swerving
rival. Then the enemy in reckless haste overtook you and, fondly
thinking that the first man [i.e. his teammate] had already gone
ahead, shamelessly made for your wheel with a sidelong dash. His
horses were brought down, a multitude of intruding legs entered the
wheels, and the twelve spokes were crowded, until a crackle came
from those crammed spaces and the revolving rim shattered the en-
tangled feet; then he, a fifth victim, flung from his chariot, which fell
upon him, caused a mountain of manifold havoc, and blood disfigured his prostrate brow.... The just emperor ordered silken
ribands to be added to the victors' palms and crowns to the necklets
of gold, and true merit to have its reward; while to the vanquished
in their sore disgrace he bade rugs of many-coloured hair to be
awarded. (Loeb Classical Library translation.)

5. Dio Chrysostom's Eulogy (28, 29)
for the Boxer Melancomas (Excerpts)

...[Melancomas] had the good fortune to be truly well-born. For
it is not because he chanced to have forbears who were rich—nay,
not even if they were kings but in other respects were quite without
merit—that this man was well-born. That term applies to those who
have come from good parents, as this man did. For his father stood
out conspicuous among all men of his time for those fairest gifts—
nobility of soul and bodily strength. This is proved by the victories
that he won, both at Olympia and in the other games.
    ...And here is an indication of the surpassing quality of his
beauty: not that he stood out pre-eminent in any company of professional men, or was admired merely by some few who saw him, no
indeed, but that he was always admired when in a company of those
who are perhaps the most beautiful men in the world—the athletes
among whom he moved. For the tallest and most comely men,
whose bodies receive the most perfect care, are these. And he was

seen by practically all mankind. For there was no city of repute, and no nation, which he did not visit; and among all alike the same opinion of him prevailed — that they had seen no one more beautiful.

...And what is most admirable in Melancomas is that, with all his beauty of figure, he surpassed in manly courage. Indeed, it seems to me that his soul vied with his body and strove to make herself the means of his winning a greater renown. He therefore, recognizing that, of all the activities conducive to courage, athletics is at once the most honourable and the most laborious, chose that. Indeed, for the soldier's career no opportunity existed, and the training also is less severe. And I for my part would venture to say that it is inferior also in that there is scope for courage alone in warfare, whereas athletics at one and the same time produce manliness, physical strength and self-control. Furthermore, he chose not the easiest branch of athletics, but the most laborious, since he trained for boxing. Now it is difficult to reach the top even in the humblest branch, let alone surpass all others in the greatest and most difficult one, as this man did.

To give the full record, one after another, of his crowns and the contests in which he won them is superfluous in the presence of you who know of them, and especially since anyone could name others who gained these same victories.... Although he met so many antagonists and such good ones, he went down before none of them, but was himself always victorious. Yet you could find in all the past no general who was never defeated, no hero in war who did not actually some time or other flee from battle. For one could not say of our friend that he remained undefeated simply because he died early, since, after all, he went through far more contests than anyone else; and the chance of losing depends upon the attempts made and not upon the length of life. Furthermore, a person might have been amazed at this — that he won all his victories without being hit or hitting his opponent, so far superior was he in strength and in his power of endurance. For often he would fight throughout the whole day, in the hottest season of the year, and although he could have more quickly won the contest by striking a blow, he refused to do it, thinking that it was possible at times for the least competent boxer to overcome by a blow the very best man, if the chance for making it were offered; but he held that it was the truest victory when he forced his opponent, although uninjured, to give up; for then the man was overcome, not by his injury, but by himself; and that for an adversary to give up because of the condition of his whole body and not simply of the part of his body that was struck, meant brilliant work on the part of the victor; whereas the man who rushed in to win as quickly as possible by striking and clinching was himself overcome by the heat and by the prolonged effort.

...So I think that under one and the same head everything has been said, not only about manliness and courage, but also about self-control and about temperance. For if Melancomas had not been self-controlled and temperate, I imagine that he would not have been so superior in strength, even if nature did make him the strongest man.

And I for my part should not hesitate to say that even of all the ancient heroes whose praises everyone chants, he possessed valour inferior to none, inferior neither to those who warred at Troy nor to those who in later times repulsed the barbarians in Greece [i.e. in the Persian invasions at Marathon in 490 and Salamis in 480]. Indeed, if he had lived in their day, his deeds would have matched theirs.

And speaking generally, I give athletics the preference over distinction in warfare on the following scores: first, that the best men in athletics would distinguish themselves in war also. . . . Second, it is not the same thing to contend against untrained opponents and men who are inferior in every way, as it is to have for one's antagonists the best men drawn from the whole inhabited earth. . . . Further, in athletics the better man proves superior to the inferior man, since he must conquer with nothing else but his courage and physical strength; while in war the might of steel, which is much superior to mere human flesh, does not allow the excellency of men's bodies to be tested and often takes the side of the inferior man. Moreover, everything that I have said about athletics I have also said about one who as an athlete, aye, and one who has been proved to be the best of the men in that profession. (Loeb Classical Library translation.)

6. Drawing Conclusions about Gladiatorial Combat from the Biographical Information

On pages 116–117 is a list of 39 gladiators as well as pertinent data about them. The following abbreviations and symbols are used:

Thr.: *Thraex*
Mur.: *murmillo*
Ess.: *essedarius*
Eq.: *eques*
Sec.: *secutor*
Ret.: *retiarius*
Con.: *contrarete*
Paeg.: *Paegniarius*
NF: not funerary
AEspA: Archivo Español de Arqueología

A dash (−) indicates that the information did not appear on the inscription, either because the inscription was fragmentary, or because the dedicator did not include it on the stone.

In the case of tombstones, the "dedicator" category refers to those who arranged for the financing and placement of the monument.

Several commonly held assumptions about gladiatorial combat can be challenged using the biographical information in the chart. Examples: (1) that most gladiatorial bouts were struggles to the death; (2) that gladiators were required to engage in matches with such frequency that their premature demise was inevitable; (3) that most gladiators were either reluctant draftees or emotionless killing machines. In fact, the biographical information will assist in demonstrating that: (1) arena fatalities of well-trained gladiators were relatively rare; (2) most gladiators fought no more than twice per year; (3) many gladiators enjoyed a strong sense of camaraderie with their fellow gladiators; also, they often married and had loyal, devoted families.

The chart regrettably represents a very small sampling of biographical data pertinent to gladiators. The fact that 35 of the 39 inscriptions are funerary will have some bearing on the nature of all the statistical information. Given these important limitations, it is rather difficult to gauge how typical these gladiators were of gladiators in general in ancient Rome. That most of the inscriptions are undated might give rise to the complaint that comparing gladiators of presumably different eras invalidates the conclusions. This is not as much of a problem as it might appear to be, however; anyone who has studied carefully the Roman gladiatorial establishment will know that dynamism was not one of its chief characteristics. Indeed, it was one of the more stagnantly conservative institutions in the history of Roman civilization. (The same might fairly be said of the Olympic games, for that matter.)

Despite these concerns, the biographies — such as they are — found on inscriptions form the most complete record which we are ever likely to receive about individual gladiators, and as such, they cannot be discounted merely on the basis of their fragmentary, incomplete or laconic nature.

An immediate question raised by the 39 biographies concerns the overall number of gladiators in the Roman world at any given time. There exist no reliable census figures to which to refer for this information, but there are a few instructive indications in some of the primary sources. According to Plutarch (*Life of Crassus* 8), the band of gladiators owned by an otherwise unnoteworthy Capuan named Lentulus Batiatus numbered at least 200 (one of whom was the more noteworthy Spartacus). There may well have been dozens,

Name of gladiator	Birthplace	Class.	Fights	Wins	Age	Dedicator(s)	Source
Alexandrinus	Macedonia	Thr.	—	—	20	Fellow Thracians	CIL 6.10197
Apollonius	—	Thr.	6	—	—	—	CIL 6.10196
Callistus	—	Thr.	—	—	20(?)	Speces, an *eques*	CIL 10.7364
Celadus	—	Thr.	—	—	—	—	CIL 4.4342
M. Ulpius Felix	Tunger	Mur.	—	—	45	Ulpia Syntache, wife; Justus, son	CIL 6.10177
Serianus Columbus	Aedua	Mur.	25(?)	—	—	Sperata, wife	CIL 5.3325
Satur	—	Mur.	13	—	—	Cornelia Severa	AEspA 33 (p. 126)
Bassus	—	Mur.	1(?)	1(?)	—	Cornelia Severa, wife	AEspA 33 (p. 126)
Cerinthus	Greece	Mur.	2	—	25	Rome, wife	AEspA 33 (p. 128)
Amandus	—	Thr.	16	—	—	NF	AEspA 33 (p. 128)
Faustus	—	Mur.	12	—	35	Apollonia, wife; Hermes, fellow Thracian	AEspA 33 (p. 130)
Probus	Germany	Mur.	—	—	49	Volumnia Sperata, wife	AE 1971 (179)
Pudens	—	Mur.	—	—	—	—	AEspA 33 (p. 128)
Beryllus	Greece	Ess.	20	—	25	Nomas, wife	CIL 12.3323
Faustus	Arabia	Ess.	—	—	37(?)	NF	CIL 12.3324
Hylas	—	Ess.	7	—	—	Ermais, wife	CIL 13.1997
Ingenuus	Germany	Ess.	—	12	25	Fellow *essedarii*	AEspA 33 (p. 131)
Maximianus Aureus	—	Sec.	5	—	22	Maximina, wife; unnamed brother	CIL 3.8830
Flamma	Syria	Sec.	34	34	30	Delicatus, a fellow gladiator	CIL 10.7297
—	Aquileia	Ret.	6	—	—	—	CIL 3.12925

Name of gladiator	Birthplace	Class.	Fights	Wins	Age	Dedicator(s)	Source
Glaucus	Mutina	Ret.	8	–	23	Aurelia, wife	CIL 5.3466
Vitalis	Batavia	Ret.	–	–	–	Himen, a fellow gladiator	CIL 11.1070
Purpurius	Greece	Ret.	11	–	–	Fellow gladiators	AE 1960 (139)
Secundus	–	Paeg.	–	–	90	Fellow gladiators	CIL 6.10168
–	–	Con.	–	44	48	Client	CIL 6.33983
Anicetus	–	Paeg.	–	–	–	Aelius Marcionus, trainer	CIL 6.10183
Cassius Victorinus	–	Ret.	–	–	35	Antonia Severa	CIL 2.499
Felix	–	Mur.	–	–	–	unnamed wife	CIL 3.8828
Amabilis	Dacia	Sec.	13	–	–		CIL 3.14644
Samus	–	Eq./Mur.	1	1	–	NF	CIL 4.4420
Pinna Columbus	–	Thr./Mur.	37	–	–	NF	CIL 4.2387
Decoratus	–	Ret./Sec.	11	–	–	Constantius, munerarius	CIL 5.563
Generosus	–	Ret.	27	27	–	–	CIL 5.3465
Urbicus	Florentia	Sec.	13	–	22	Lauricia, wife, and daughter	CIL 5.5933
Lycus	–	Mur.	4	–	–	Longinas, brother	CIL 6.10180
T. Flavius Incitatus	–	Sec.	16	–	27	–	CIL 6.10189
Marcus Antonius Niger	–	Thr.	18	–	38	–	CIL 6.10195
Jantinus	Phrygia	Ret.	5	–	24	Ingenua, wife	CIL 5.4506
Pardonus	Dertona	–	11	–	27	Arriane, wife	CIL 5.3468

perhaps hundreds of similarly outfitted owners of gladiators throughout Italy. In his autobiography, Augustus proclaims that 10,000 gladiators fought at the shows he sponsored. According to Suetonius (*Life of Nero* 12), 400 senators and 600 equestrians donned gladiatorial gear in one of Nero's shows. Hence, it seems not unreasonable to conclude that in the late Republic and early Empire, there were thousands of men — indeed, probably tens of thousands — engaged as gladiators.

Since the vast majority of these gladiators certainly ended their careers with discharges rather than death, their average life-span would have been greater than that of the gladiators represented on the chart, since 90 percent of those were presumably killed in the arena. Even so, the average age at death for the 21 gladiators whose ages appear on their epitaphs is 32.8. Even if the 90-year-old Secundus is eliminated, the average is still nearly 30. If one assumes — as many classical scholars would — that the life expectancy for an ancient Roman was about 35, it would appear that gladiators could have hoped to enjoy a life span comparable to that of their nongladiatorial contemporaries. For although a gladiatorial career involved obvious risks, it also offered substantial benefits contributing to an increased life expectancy: decent food; good accommodations; top-notch coaching; emphasis on physical fitness and training; competent if not excellent medical care. (Indeed, many young physicians acquired their first practical experiences in medicine by treating wounded gladiators. Marcus Aurelius' noted doctor, Galen, began his career as a staff physician at a gladiatorial school.)

For 25 of the 39 gladiators, the number of fights is recorded, ranging from one to 37; the average is about 13. This supports the view that the typical gladiatorial match did not conclude with the death of one of the combatants.

In 11 cases, both the number of fights and the age at death appear; the approximate averages are, respectively, 13 (as mentioned) and 27. If one assumes that these 11 gladiators began their careers in their late teens — a reasonable assumption based on the available evidence — then it is clear that they averaged fewer than two fights per year. It is highly likely that this figure was the norm for most gladiators.

Even the most cursory scanning of the birthplaces of these gladiators graphically illustrates the international nature of the institution. While many gladiators hailed from Italy, they also came from Gaul, Germany, Greece and even as far away as Syria and

Arabia. Interestingly, of the 17 gladiators whose birthplaces are listed not one came from Rome itself.

Gladiatorial classification is the most commonly recorded biographical item, appearing in 38 of the 39 cases under consideration. Yet in only three instances is more than one classification listed, thus suggesting that gladiators remained in the same category for the duration of their careers.

On 27 of the 35 epitaphs, the name(s) of those who dedicated the monument appear, usually the relatives or friends of the deceased. This feature more than any other tends to humanize an institution that is generally seen as mercilessly brutal. Most gladiators seem to have had a very strong support network composed of their families and even their fellow gladiators. It is very probable that a sort of camaraderie developed among these men, who spent much of their waking hours training together in a common enterprise. The spirit of mutual respect and friendship undoubtedly encompassed even those gladiators who would be pitted against one another in the arena.

7. How Long Was Diocles' Career?

The standard interpretation of the words *summa quadriga agitavit annis XXIIII* (in line six of the Diocles inscription) has always been: "Summary: he drove a chariot for 24 years." An alternative translation would be: "He drove for his chief faction [the Reds] for 24 years," understanding *quadriga* as faction rather than chariot, and *summa* as an adjective, not a noun. This presumes a metonymical translation of *quadriga* as faction, and as there are no corroborative parallel passages elsewhere in Latin, it would seem that this interpretation is doomed. Nevertheless, a case for its accuracy can be made.

An examination of the content of line eleven reveals the words *eripuit et vicit DII prasinis CCXVI venetis CCV albatis LXXXI:* "He snatched away victory 502 times: from the Greens, 216; from the Blues, 205; from the Whites, 81." Why no mention of the Reds? After all, Diocles raced against them for fully nine years as a member of the other factions. Could it be plausibly argued that in those nine years, he never won an *eripuit* victory against the Reds? Hardly.

It must be assumed, therefore, that all 502 *eripuit* wins came while he wore the red tunic. If that be the case, then internal consistency demands a similar interpretation for the other statistics presented in this section: i.e., that the 815 *occupavit* wins, the 67 *successit*, the 36 *praemisit*, and the 42 *varii* were all gained by Diocles while a member of the Red faction, or 1,462 in all. Hence, his career total would be not 1,462, but 1,563, adding the ten wins for the Blue faction and the 91 for the White mentioned in line nine. (The phrases *ad venetum* and *ad albatum* do mean *for* [not against, as some would have it] the Blue and White, respectively.)

Other questions should be considered. Why, for example, do the words *factionis russatae* (of the Red faction) appear so prominently in the first line, especially since Diocles drove for all four factions at one point or another in his career? Clearly, this inscription is meant to glorify the Red faction as much as it is Diocles. Indeed, it is possible — likely, even — that the faction financed the making of the plaque. If so, then it would make sense contextually, if not philologically, to understand *summa quadriga* as "chief faction": the Reds.

The only truly genuine counterargument would focus on chronology: if Diocles raced chariots for 33 (not 24) years, and retired at age 42, it would, of course, follow that he began at age nine. This is not as farfetched as it may seem, however; drivers not infrequently embarked upon their careers at a very young age. One need look no further for corroboration than the plaintive epitaph of the child-driver Florus (*see* that entry, page 59).

V. Lists of Athletes and Horses

1. Eusebius' List of Stade Race Winners

Olympiad	Date	Winner/place of origin
1	776	Coroebus of Elis
2	772	Antimachus of Elis
3	768	Androclus of Messenia
4	764	Polychares of Messenia
5	760	Aeschines of Elis
6	756	Oebotas of Dyme
7	752	Diocles of Messenia
8	748	Anticles of Messenia
9	744	Xenocles of Messenia
10	740	Dotades of Messenia
11	736	Leochares of Messenia
12	732	Oxythemis of Cleonae
13	728	Diocles of Corinth
14	724	Desmon of Corinth
15	720	Orhippus of Megara
16	716	Pythagoras of Sparta
17	712	Polus of Epidaurus
18	708	Tellus of Sicyon
19	704	Menos of Megara
20	700	Atheradas of Sparta
21	696	Pantacles of Athens
22	692	Pantacles of Athens
23	688	Icarius of Hiperesia
24	684	Cleoptilomaeus of Sparta
25	680	Thalpis of Sparta
26	676	Callisthenes of Sparta
27	672	Eurybos of Athens
28	668	Charmis of Sparta
29	664	Chionis of Sparta
30	660	Chionis of Sparta
31	656	Chionis of Sparta
32	652	Cratinus of Megara

Olympiad	Date	Winner/place of origin
33	648	Gylis of Sparta
34	644	Stomus of Athens
35	640	Sphaerus of Sparta
36	636	Phrynon of Athens
37	632	Euryclidas of Sparta
38	628	Olyntheus of Sparta
39	624	Rhipsolaus of Sparta
40	620	Olyntheus of Sparta
41	616	Cleondas of Thebes
42	612	Lycotas of Sparta
43	608	Cleon of Epidaurus
44	604	Gelon of Sparta
45	600	Anticrates of Epidaurus
46	596	Chrysamachus of Sparta
47	592	Eurycles of Sparta
48	588	Glycon of Croton
49	584	Lycinus of Croton
50	580	Epitelidas of Sparta
51	576	Eratosthenes of Croton
52	572	Agis of Elis
53	568	Hagnon of Peparethus
54	564	Hippostratus of Croton
55	560	Hippostratus of Croton
56	556	Phaedrus of Pharsalia
57	552	Lagramus of Sparta
58	548	Diognetus of Croton
59	544	Archilochus of Corcyra
60	540	Apelleius of Elis
61	536	Agatharchus of Corcyra
62	532	Erixias of Chalcidice
63	528	Parmenides of Camarina
64	524	Menander of Thessaly
65	520	Anochus of Tarentum
66	516	Ischyrus of Himera
67	512	Phanus of Pellana
68	508	Isomachus of Croton
69	504	Isomachus of Croton
70	500	Nicasius of Opus
71	496	Tisicrates of Croton
72	492	Tisicrates of Croton
73	488	Astylus of Croton
74	484	Astylus of Croton
75	480	Astylus of Croton
76	476	Scamander of Mitylene
77	472	Dandes of Argos
78	468	Parmenides of Posidonia
79	464	Xenophon of Corinth
80	460	Torimmas of Thessaly

Olympiad	Date	Winner/place of origin
81	456	Paulimastus of Cyrene
82	452	Licus of Larissa
83	448	Crison of Himera
84	444	Crison of Himera
85	440	Crison of Himera
86	436	Theopompus of Thessaly
87	432	Sophron of Ambracia
88	428	Symmachus of Messana (Sicily)
89	424	Symmachus of Messana (Sicily)
90	420	Hyperbius of Syracuse
91	416	Exagentus of Acragas
92	412	Exagentus of Acragas
93	408	Eurotus of Cyrene
94	404	Crocinas of Larissa
95	400	Minon of Athens
96	396	Eupolemus of Elis
97	392	Tirinaeus of Elis [?]
98	388	Sosippus of Delphi
99	384	Dicon of Syracuse
100	380	Dionysidorus of Tarentum
101	376	Damon of Thurii
102	372	Damon of Thurii
103	368	Pethostratus of Ephesus
104	364	Phocides of Athens
105	360	Porus of Cyrene
106	356	Porus of Cyrene
107	352	Micrinas of Tarentum
108	348	Polycles of Cyrene
109	344	Aristolochus of Athens
110	340	Anicles of Athens
111	336	Cleomantis of Clitor
112	332	Eurylas of Chalcidice
113	328	Cliton of Macedonia
114	324	Micinas of Rhodes
115	320	Damasias of Amphipolis
116	316	Demosthenes of Sparta
117	312	Parmenides of Mitylene
118	308	Andromenes of Corinth
119	304	Andromenes of Corinth
120	300	Pythagoras of Magnesia (Maeander)
121	296	Pythagoras of Magnesia (Maeander)
122	292	Antigonus of Macedonia
123	288	Antigonus of Macedonia
124	284	Philomelus of Pharsalia
125	280	Ladas of Aegae
126	276	Idaeus or Nicator of Cyrene
127	272	Perigenes of Alexandria
128	268	Seleucus of Macedonia

Olympiad	Date	Winner/place of origin
129	264	Philinus of Cos
130	260	Philinus of Cos
131	256	Ammonius of Alexandria
132	252	Xenophanes of Aetolia
133	248	Simelus of Naples
134	244	Alcides of Sparta
135	240	Eraton of Aetolia
136	236	Pythocles of Sicyon
137	232	Menestheus of Bargylia
138	228	Demetrius of Alexandria
139	224	Iolaedas of Argos
140	220	Zopirus of Syracuse
141	216	Dorotheus of Rhodes
142	212	Crates of Alexandria
143	208	Heraclitus of Samos
144	204	Heraclitus of Salamis on the island of Cyprus
145	200	Pyrrhias of Aetolia
146	196	Micion of Boeotia
147	192	Agemachus of Cyzicus
148	188	Archesilaus of Megalopolis
149	184	Hippostratus of Seleucia
150	180	Onesicratus of Salamis (whether the island or the Cypriot city is uncertain; Moretti suggests the latter)
151	176	Thymilus of Aspendus
152	172	Democrates of Megara
153	168	Aristandrus of Lesbos
154	164	Leonidas of Rhodes
155	160	Leonidas of Rhodes
156	156	Leonidas of Rhodes
157	152	Leonidas of Rhodes
158	148	Orthon of Syracuse
159	144	Alcimus of Cyzicus
160	140	Anodorus of Cyzicus
161	136	Antipater of Epirus
162	132	Damon of Delphi
163	128	Timotheus of Tralles
164	124	Boeotus of Sicyon
165	120	Acusilaus of Cyrene
166	116	Chrysogonus of Nicaea
167	112	Chrysogonus of Nicaea
168	108	Nicomachus of Philadelphia
169	104	Nicodemus of Sparta
170	100	Simmias of Seleucia
171	96	Parmeniscus of Corcyra
172	92	Eudamus of Cos
173	88	Parmeniscus of Corcyra

Olympiad	Date	Winner/place of origin
174	84	Demostratus of Larissa
175	80	Epaenetus of Argos
176	76	Dio of Cyprus
177	72	Hecatomnus of Elis
178	68	Diocles of Hypaepa
179	64	Andreas of Sparta
180	60	Andromachus of Sparta
181	56	Lamachus of Tauromenium
182	52	Anestion of Argos
183	48	Theodorus of Messenia
184	44	Theodorus of Messenia
185	40	Ariston of Thurii
186	36	Scamander of Alexandria (Troad)
187	32	Ariston of Thurii
188	28	Sopratus of Argos
189	24	Asclepiades of Sicyon
190	20	Auphidius of Patrae
191	16	Diodotus of Tyana
192	12	Diophanes of Aeolia
193	8	Artemidorus of Thyatira
194	4 B.C.	Demaratus of Ephesus

(Given that there is no year "zero," the 195th Olympiad is considered to have been held in the year A.D. 1.)

Olympiad	Date	Winner/place of origin
195	A.D. 1	Demaratus of Ephesus
196	5	Pammenes of Magnesia (Maeander)
197	9	Asiaticus of Halicarnassus
198	13	Diophanes of Prusa
199	17	Aeschines of Miletus
200	21	Polemon of Petra
201	25	Damasias of Cydonia (Crete)
202	29	Hermogenes of Pergamum
203	33	Apollonius of Epidaurus
204	37	Sarapion of Alexandria
205	41	Eubulidas of Laodicaea
206	45	Valerius of Mitylene
207	49	Athenodorus of Aegium
208	53	Athenodorus of Aegium
209	57	Callicles of Sidon
210	61	Athenodorus of Aegium
211	65 (or 67?)	Triphon of Philadelphia; according to Eusebius and others, the 211th Olympiad was postponed until A.D. 67, because of the emperor Nero's failure to arrive in Olympia in 65 in time.
212	69	Polites of Ceramus
213	73	Rhodon of Cyme

Olympiad	Date	Winner/place of origin
214	77	Straton of Alexandria
215	81	Hermogenes of Xanthus
216	85	Apollophanes of Tarsus
217	89	Hermogenes of Xanthus
218	93	Apollonis of Alexandria
219	97	Stephanus of Cappadocia
220	101	Achilles of Alexandria
221	105	Theonas of Alexandria
222	109	Callistus of Side
223	113	Eustolus of Side
224	117	Isarion of Alexandria
225	121	Aristeas of Miletus
226	125	Dionysius of Alexandria
227	129	Dionysius of Alexandria
228	133	Lycas of Alexandria
229	137	Epidaurus of Alexandria
230	141	Didymus of Alexandria
231	145	Cranaus of Sicyon
232	149	Atticus of Sardinia
233	153	Demetrius of Chios
234	157	Eras of Chios
235	161	Mnesibulus of Elatea
236	165	Aethales of Alexandria
237	169	Eudaemon of Alexandria
238	173	Agathopus of Aegina
239	177	Agathopus of Aegina
240	181	Anubion of Alexandria
241	185	Heron of Alexandria
242	189	Magnus Libicus of Cyrene
243	193	Isodorus of Alexandria
244	197	Isodorus of Alexandria
245	201	Alexander of Alexandria
246	205	Epinicus of Cyzicus
247	209	Satornilus of Gortyna (Crete)
248	213	Heliodorus of Alexandria
249	217	Heliodorus of Alexandria

2. Athletes for Whom Pindar Wrote Epinicean Odes

Winner/place of origin	Event	Ode(s)
Alcimedon of Aegina	wrestling (boys')	*Olympian* 8
Alcimidas of Aegina	wrestling (boys')	*Nemean* 6
Arcesilas of Cyrene	chariot race	*Pythian* 4, 5
Aristoclides of Aegina	pankration	*Nemean* 3
Aristomenes of Aegina	wrestling (boys')	*Pythian* 8

Winner/place of origin	Event	Ode(s)
Asopichus of Orchomenus	stade (boys')	*Olympian* 14
Chromius of Aetna	chariot race	*Nemean* 1
Cleander of Aegina	pankration (boys'?)	*Isthmian* 8
Diagoras of Rhodes	boxing	*Olympian* 7
Dinias of Aegina	diaulos	*Nemean* 8
Epharmostus of Opus	wrestling	*Olympian* 9
Ergoteles of Himera	dolichos	*Olympian* 12
Hagesias of Syracus	chariot race	*Olympian* 6
Hagesidamus of Western Locri	boxing (boys')	*Olympian* 10, 11
Herodotus of Thebes	chariot race	*Isthmian* 1
Hieron of Aetna	chariot race	*Pythian* 1
Hieron of Syracuse	horse, chariot race	*Olympian* 1; *Pythian* 2, 3
Hippocleas of Thessaly	diaulos (boys')	*Pythian* 10
Megacles of Athens	chariot race	*Pythian* 7
Melissus of Thebes*	pankration (?) chariot race (?)	*Isthmian* 3, 4
Phylacidas of Aegina	pankration	*Isthmian* 5, 6
Psaumis of Camarina	chariot race	*Olympian* 4, 5
Pytheas of Aegina	pankration (boys')	*Nemean* 5
Sogenes of Aegina	pentathlon (boys')	*Nemean* 7
Strepsiades of Thebes	pankration	*Isthmian* 7
Telesicrates of Cyrene	hoplite race	*Pythian* 9
Theaeus of Argos	wrestling	*Nemean* 10
Theron of Acragas	chariot race	*Olympian* 2, 3
Thrasydalus of Thebes	stade (boys')	*Pythian* 11
Timasarchus of Aegina	wrestling (boys')	*Nemean* 4
Timodemus of Acharnae	pankration	*Nemean* 2
Xenocrates of Acragas	chariot race	*Pythian* 6; *Isthmian* 2
Xenophon of Corinth	stade/pentathlon	*Olympian* 13

* *See Special Essay 1, pages 102–103*

3. Athletes Cited in Books 5 and 6 of Pausanias

An asterisk (*) after an event indicates that the athlete won championships in both the boys' and men's divisions (but not in same Olympiad).

Athlete/place of origin	Event	Reference
Acanthus of Sparta	dolichos	5.8.6
Acusilaus of Rhodes	boxing (boys')	6.7.1,3
Aeschines of Elis	pentathlon	6.14.13
Aesypus [origin not stated]	horse race	6.2.8
Agathinus of Elis	not stated	6.13.11
Ageles of Chios	boxing (boys')	6.15.2

Athlete/place of origin	Event	Reference
Agemetor of Mantinea	boxing (boys')	6.9.9
Agenor of Thebes	wrestling (boys')	6.6.2
Agesarchus of Tritaea	boxing	6.12.8
Agiadas of Elis	boxing (boys')	6.10.9
Alcaenetus of Leprae	boxing	6.7.8
Alcetus of Clitor	boxing (boys')	6.9.2
Alexibius of Heraea	pentathlon	6.17.4
Alexinicus of Elis	wrestling (boys')	6.17.7
Amertes of Elis	wrestling*	6.8.1
Amyntas of Ephesus	pankration (boys')	6.4.5
Anauchidas of Elis	wrestling*	6.14.11; 6.16.1
Anaxander of Sparta	chariot race	6.1.7
Androsthenes of Maenalus	pankration	6.6.1
Anochus of Tarentum	stade/diaulos	6.14.11
Antigonus of Elis	not stated	6.16.2
Antiochus of Leprae	pentathlon/pankration	6.3.9
Antipater of Miletus	boxing (boys')	6.2.6
Aratus of Sicyon	chariot race	6.12.5, 6; *see also* 2.8
Arcesilaus of Sparta	chariot race	6.2.2
Archedamus of Elis	wrestling (boys')	6.1.3
Archidamus of Elis	chariot race	6.17.5
Archippus of Mitylene	boxing	6.15.1
Aristeus of Argos	dolichos	6.9.3
Aristides of Elis	diaulos/hoplite race dolichos (boys')	6.16.4–5
Aristion of Epidaurus	boxing	6.13.6
Aristodemus of Elis	boxing	6.3.4
Artemidorus of Tralles	pankration	6.14.3
Asamon of Elis	boxing	6.16.5
Astylus of Croton	stade/diaulos	6.13.1
Athenaeus of Ephesus	boxing (boys')	6.4.1
Baucis of Troezen	wrestling	6.8.4
Belistiche of Macedonia	chariot race	5.8.11
Brimias of Elis	boxing	6.16.5
Butas of Miletus	boxing (boys')	6.17.3
Bycelus of Sicyon	boxing (boys')	6.13.7
Callias of Athens	pankration	6.6.1
Callicrates of Magnesia (Lethaeus)	hoplite race	6.17.3
Calliteles of Sparta	wrestling	6.16.6
Callon of Elis	boxing (boys')	6.12.6
Caprus of Elis	wrestling/pankration boxing*	6.15.4–5, 10; 6.16.1
Chaereas of Sicyon	boxing (boys')	6.3.1
Charinus of Elis	diaulos/hoplite race	6.15.2
Charmides of Elis	boxing (boys')	6.7.1
Chilon of Patrae	wrestling	6.4.6–7

Athlete/Place of origin	Event	Reference
Chimon of Argos	wrestling	6.9.3
Chionis of Sparta	stade/diaulos; hoplite (?)	6.13.2; see also 3.14.3; 4.23.4, 10
Choerilus of Elis	boxing (boys')	6.17.5
Clearetus of Elis	pentathlon	6.16.9
Cleogenes of Elis	horse race	6.1.4
Cleomedes of Astypalaea	boxing	6.9.6-8
Cleosthenes of Epidamnus	chariot race	6.10.6-8
Clinomachus of Elis	pentathlon	6.15.1
Clitomachus of Thebes	wrestling/boxing pankration	6.15.3-5
Coroebus of Elis	stade	5.8.6; see also 8.26.3-4
Cratinus of Aegira	wrestling (boys')	6.3.6
Cratisthenes of Cyrene	chariot race	6.18.1
Crauxidas of Crannon	horse race	5.8.8
Criannius of Elis	hoplite race	6.17.1
Critodamus of Clitor	boxing (boys')	6.8.5
Crocon of Eretria	horse race	6.14.4
Cynisca of Sparta	chariot race	5.12.5; 6.1.6; see also 3.8. 1-2; 3.15.1
Damagetus of Rhodes	pankration	6.7.1,3
Damarchus of Parrhasia	boxing	6.8.2
Damaretus of Heraea	hoplite race	5.8.10; 6.10.4
Damaretus of Messenia	boxing (boys')	6.14.11
Damiscus of Messenia	stade (boys')/ pentathlon	6.2.10-11
Damoxenidas of Maenalus	boxing	6.6.3
Democrates of Tenedos	wrestling	6.17.1
Diagoras of Rhodes	boxing	6.7.1-4
Diallus of Smyrna	pankration (boys')	6.13.6
Dicon of Caulonia	stade	6.3.11
Dinolochus of Elis	foot race (boys')	6.1.5
Dinosthenes of Sparta	stade	6.16.8
Dorieus of Rhodes	pankration	6.7.1,4-6
Dromeus of Mantinea	pankration	6.11.4
Dromeus of Stymphalus	dolichos	6.7.10
Eicasius of Colophon	wrestling (boys')	6.17.4
Enation [origin not stated]	stade (boys')	6.17.4
Eperastus of Elis	hoplite race	6.17.5-6
Epicradius of Mantinea	boxing (boys')	6.10.9
Epitherses of Erythrae	boxing	6.15.6
Ergoteles of Cnossus	dolichos	6.4.11
Euagoras of Elis	chariot race	5.8.10
Euagoras of Sparta	chariot race	6.10.8
Eualcidas of Elis	boxing (boys')	6.16.6

Athlete/place of origin	Event	Reference
Euanoridas of Elis	wrestling (boys')	6.8.1
Euanthes of Cyzicus	boxing	6.4.10
Eubotas of Cyrene	stade/chariot race	6.8.3
Eucles of Rhodes	boxing	6.6.2; 6.7.2
Eupolemus of Elis	stade/pentathlon	6.3.7
Eurybatus of Sparta	wrestling	5.8.7
Eutelidas of Sparta	wrestling (boys')	5.9.1; 6.15.8
	pentathlon (boys')	
Euthymenes of Maenalus	wrestling*	6.8.5
Euthymus of Western Locri	boxing	6.6.4–11;
		6.11.4
Gelon [origin not stated]	chariot race	6.9.4–5
Glaucon of Athens	chariot race	6.16.9
Glaucus of Carystus	boxing	6.10.1–3
Gnathon of Maenalus	boxing (boys')	6.7.9
Gorgus of Elis	pentathlon/diaulos/	6.15.9
	hoplite race	
Gorgus of Messenia	pentathlon	6.14.11
Hellanicus of Leprae	boxing (boys')	6.7.8
Hermesianax of Colophon	wrestling (boys')	6.17.4
Hermogenes of Xanthus	foot racer	6.13.3
Herodotus of Clazomenia	stade (boys')	6.17.2
Hieron of Syracuse	chariot race	6.12.1
Hieronymus of Andros	pentathlon	6.14.13
Hippomachus of Elis	boxing (boys')	6.12.6
Hipposthenes* of Sparta	wrestling (boys')	5.8.9
Hippus of Elis	boxing (boys')	6.3.5
Hypenus of Pisa	diaulos	5.8.6
Hysmon of Elis	pentathlon	6.3.9–10
Iccus of Epidaurus	boxing	6.9.6
Iccus of Tarentum	pentathlon	6.10.5
Idaeus of Cyrene	stade	6.12.2
Labax of Elis	boxing	6.3.4
Lampis of Sparta	pentathlon	5.8.7
Lampus of Macedonia	chariot race	6.4.10
Lastratidas of Elis	wrestling (boys')	6.6.3
Leon of Ambracia	stade	6.3.7
Leonidas of Naxos	not stated	6.16.5
Leonidas of Rhodes	stade/diaulos/	6.13.4
	dolichos	
Leontiscus of Messana (Sicily)	wrestling	6.4.3
Lichas of Sparta	chariot race	6.2.2–3
Lycinus of Elis	boxing (boys')	6.7.9
Lycinus of Heraea	stade (boys')	6.10.9
Lycinus of Sparta	chariot race	6.2.2
Lygdamis of Syracuse	pankration	5.8.8
Lysander of Sparta	not stated	6.3.14
Lysippus of Elis	wrestling (boys')	6.16.7

Athlete/place of origin	Event	Reference
Menacles of Elis	pentathlon	6.16.5
Meneptolemus of Apollonia	stade (boys')	6.14.13
Milo of Croton	wrestler	6.14.5–9
Miltiades of Athens	chariot race	6.10.8; 6.19.6
Mnaseas of Cyrene	hoplite race	6.13.7; 6.18.1
Molpion [origin not stated]	not stated	6.4.8
Myron of Sicyon	chariot race	6.19.1–2, 4
Narycidas of Phigalia	wrestling	6.6.1
Neolaidas of Elis	stade/hoplite race	6.16.8
Neolaidas of Pheneus	boxing (boys')	6.1.3
Nicander of Elis	stade/diaulos	6.16.5
Nicasylus of Rhodes	wrestling	6.14.2
Nicostratus of Heraea	wrestling (boys')	6.3.11
Oebotas of Dyme	stade	6.3.8; *see also* 7.17.6; 8.17.13–14
Olidas of Elis	not stated	6.15.2
Onomastus of Smyrna	boxing	5.8.7
Paeanius of Elis	wrestling	6.15.10; 6.16.9
Pagondas of Thebes	chariot race	5.8.7
Pantarces of Elis	wrestling (boys')	6.10.6
Pantarces of Elis	horse race	6.15.2
Paraballon of Elis	diaulos	6.6.3
Pataecus of Dyme	horse race	5.8.11
Pherenicus of Elis	wrestling (boys')	6.16.1
Pherias of Aegina	wrestling (boys')	6.14.1
Phidimus of Troas	pankration (boys')	5.8.11
Phidolas of Corinth	horse race	6.13.9–10
Philinus of Cos	foot race	6.17.2
Philippus of Pellana	boxing (boys')	6.8.5
Philles of Elis	wrestling (boys')	6.9.4
Philon of Corcyra	boxing	6.9.9
Philon of Corcyra	stade (boys')	6.14.13
Philonides of Chersonesus	not stated	6.16.5
Philytas of Sybaris	boxing (boys')	5.8.9
Pisirodus of Rhodes	boxing (boys')	6.7.2,4
Plistaenus of Aetolia	not stated	6.16.1
Polites of Ceramus	stade/diaulos/ dolichos	6.13.3–4
Polycles [origin not stated]	chariot race	6.1.7
Polydamas of Scotussa	pankration	6.5.1, 4–9
Polynices of Elis	stade (boys')	5.8.9
Polypithes of Sparta	chariot race	6.16.6
Praxidamas of Aegina	boxing	6.18.7
Procles of Andros	wrestling (boys')	6.14.13
Promachus of Pellana	pankration	6.8.6; *see also* 7.27.5
Protolaus of Mantinea	boxing (boys')	6.6.1

Athlete/place of origin	Event	Reference
Ptolemy [origin not stated]	horse race (?)	6.16.9; 6.17.3
Pyrilampes of Ephesus	dolichos	6.3.13
Pytharchus of Mantinea	stade (boys')	6.7.1
Pythocles of Elis	pentathlon	6.7.10
Pyttalus of Elis	boxing (boys')	6.16.8
Satyrus of Elis	boxing	6.4.5
Scaeus of Samos	boxing (boys')	6.13.5
Seleadas of Sparta	wrestling	6.16.6
Seleucus of Elis	not stated	6.16.2
Socrates of Pellana	stade (boys')	6.8.1
Sodamas of Assus	stade (boys')	6.4.9
Sophius of Messenia	stade (boys')	6.3.2
Sostratus of Sicyon	pankration	6.4.1–3
Sotades of Crete	dolichos	6.18.6
Stomius of Elis	pentathlon	6.3.2–3
Sybariades of Sparta	chariot race	5.8.10
Symmachus of Elis	wrestling	6.1.3
Taurosthenes of Aegina	wrestling	6.9.3
Telemachus of Elis	chariot race	6.13.11
Telestas of Messenia	boxing (boys')	6.14.4
Tellon of Oresthas	boxing (boys')	6.10.9
Theagenes of Thasos	boxing/pankration/ dolichos	6.6.5–6; 6.11. 2–9; 6.15.3
Theantus of Leprae	boxing (boys')	6.7.8
Theochrestus of Cyrene	chariot race	6.12.7
Theodorus of Elis	pentathlon	6.16.8
Theognetus of Aegina	wrestling (boys')	6.9.1
Theopompus of Heraea	pentathlon	6.10.4
Theopompus of Heraea	wrestling	6.10.4–5
Theotimus of Elis	boxing (boys')	6.17.5
Thersilochus of Corcyra	boxing (boys')	6.13.6
Thersius of Thessaly	chariot race	5.9.1
Timanthes of Cleonae	pankration	6.8.4
Timasitheus of Croton	wrestling	6.14.5
Timasitheus of Delphi	pankration	6.8.6
Timon [origin not stated]	chariot race	6.2.8
Timon of Elis	chariot race	6.12.6
Timon of Elis	pentathlon	6.16.2
Timosthenes of Elis	stade (boys')	6.2.6
Tisamenus of Elis	pentathlon	6.14.13; see also 3.11.6
Tisander of Naxos	boxing	6.13.8
Tlepolemus of Lycaea	horse race	5.8.11
Troilus of Elis	chariot race	6.1.4–5
Xenarces of Stratus	pankration	6.2.1
Xenocles of Maenalus	wrestling (boys')	6.9.2
Xenodicus [origin not stated]	boxing (boys')	6.14.12
Xenombrotus of Cos	horse race	6.14.12

Athlete/place of origin	Event	Reference
Xenon of Leprae	stade (boys')	6.15.1
Xenophon of Aegium	pankration	6.3.13

4. The Lycaean Victor List (Syll³ 314)

An inscription from Lycaea is Asia Minor records the names of the winners of the various events of the quadrennial Lycaean festival, from 320 to 304.

[Winners in 320:]

Event	Name/hometown of winner
Two-horse chariot	Dameas of Lycaea
Four-horse chariot (colts)	Eupolemus of Arcadia
Four-horse chariot (horses)	Chionidas of Arcadia
Horse race	Philonicus of Argos
Stade (boys')	Theoteles of Arcadia
Wrestling (boys')	Thrasydemus of Athens
Boxing (boys')	Nicias of Arcadia
Dolichos (men's)	Aristippus of Arcadia
Stade (men's)	Lysilochus of Argos
Diaulos (men's)	Dinon of Arcadia
Wrestling (men's)	Aristomenes of Argos
Pentathlon	Hagesistratus of Argos
Boxing (men's)	Andromachus of Lycaea
Pankration (men's)	Antenor of Miletus
Hoplite race	Pantichus of Arcadia

[Winners in 316:]

Dolichos (men's)	Aristippus of Arcadia
Stade (boys')	Dinias of Arcadia
Stade (men's)	Aristodamus of Argos
Diaulos (men's)	Archedamus of Argos
Pentathlon (men's)	Androbius of Sparta
Hoplite race (men's)	Amyander of Acarnania
Wrestling (men's [or boys'?])*	Isagenes of Arcadia
Wrestling (men's [or boys'?])*	Selidas of Sparta
Boxing (boys')	Diullus of Arcadia
Boxing (men's)	Dieuches of Arcadia
Pankration (men's)	Euanor of Arcadia
Two-horse chariot	Amphinetus of Arcadia
Horse race	Pasicles of Sparta

[Winners in 312:]

Dolichos (men's)	Pistagoras of Arcadia

[The rest of this section is fragmentary.]

Event	Name/hometown of winner
	[Winners in 308:]
Two-horse chariot	Dagus of Macedonia
Four-horse chariot (colts)	Damolytus of Lycaea
Horse race	Onomantus of Argos
Four-horse chariot (horses)	Epinetus of Macedonia
Dolichos (men's)	Ageus (of Argos?)

[This section of the inscription is also quite fragmentary.]

	[Winners in 304:]
Stade (boys')	Tellias of Arcadia
Stade (men's)	Heraclitus of Macedonia
Pentathlon	Alexibius of Arcadia
Dolichos (men's)	Philistidas of Argos
Diaulos (men's)	Philocrates of Syracuse
Wrestling (boys')	Theoteles of Arcadia
Boxing (boys')	Theogiton of Arcadia
Wrestling (men's)	Aristodamus of Argos
Boxing (men's)	Timodorus of Arcadia
Pankration (men's)	Aristonymus of Argos
Hoplite race (men's)	Philocrates of Syracuse
Two-horse chariot	Nicagoras of Rhodes
Four-horse chariot (colts)	Thearidas of Arcadia
Horse race	Bubalus of Cassandria

5. Three Lists from Oropus

An inscribed tablet discovered near Oropus includes the names of several athletes and the events in which they competed. No other information (e.g. pertaining to their statistics) appears. The *IG* editors have dated the inscription to the fourth century primarily on the basis of the shapes and appearance of the lettering. The names of a flute and lyre player appear first, followed by the name of a *sophistes*, "master musician."

Name	Place of origin	Event
Pausimachus	Athens	Dolichos (boys')
Mnesarchides	Athens	Dolichos (men's)
Malacus	Macedonia	Stade (boys', to which the phrase *ex hapanton*, "out of many," is appended.)
Theopompus	Cyrene	Stade (youth's)
Acarnan	Athens	Stade (men's)
Anthippus	Argos	Diaulos (boys'), *ex hapanton*
Epicrates	Larissa	Pentathlon (youth's)
Hieron	Argos	Diaulos (men's)
Thasyaner	Colophon	Horse race (boys')
Mnesarchides	Athens	Horse race (men's)
Thasyaner	Colophon	Wrestling (boys'), *ex hapanton*

Name	Place of origin	Event
Aristichmus	Andros	Wrestling (youth's)
Philonicus	Argos	Pankration (boys')
Antiphanes	Athens	Wrestling (men's)
Eutelion	Phlius	Boxing (men's)
Satyrus	Elis	Pankration (youth's)
Stratocles	Athens	Boxing (boys')
Pausias	Athens	Pentathlon (men's)
Melanippus	Pharsalia	Hoplite race
Anthippus	Argos	Stade (boys', to which the phrase *apo gymnasion,* "from the gymnasion," is appended.)
Antibius	Athens	Wrestling (boys'), *apo gymnasion*
Charisander	Athens	Boxing (boys'), *apo gymnasion*
Nicodemus	Athens	Pankration (boys'), *apo gymnasion*

[Several other athletes were apparently listed, but the inscription at this point becomes too fragmentary to ascertain their names.]

Another inscription (*IG* 7.417) from Oropus, dated by its editors to the first century:

In the athletic contests:

Name	Place of origin	Event
Euarchus	Coronea	Dolichos (boys')
Parmeniscus	Corcyra	Dolichos (men's)
Asclepiades	Heraclitus	Stade (boys')
Callon	Opus	Stade (youth's)
Craton	Hyettus	Stade (men's)
Nicocles	Sparta	Diaulos (boys')
Parmeniscus	Corcyra	Diaulos (men's)
Nicocles	Sparta	Horse race (boys')
Asopichus	Thebes	Horse race (men's)
Dexias	Epidamnus	Pentathlon (boys')
Xenon	Thebes	Pentathlon (youth's)
Diogenes	[not extant]	Pentathlon (men's)
Artemidorus	[not extant]	Wrestling (boys')
Habrias	Sparta	Wrestling (youth's)
Straton	Smyrna	Wrestling (men's)
Leucinas	Thebes	Boxing (boys')
Eucrates	[not extant]	Boxing (youth's)
Glaucias	Tyre	Boxing (men's)
Attinas	Cyme	Pankration (boys')
Eucharidas	[not fully extant; restored as Opus by the editors.]	Pankration (youth's)
Leucinas [see note 3, infra]	Thebes	Pankration (men's)
Atinas [sic]	Cyme	Hoplite race

Name	Place of origin	Event
	In the equestrian contests:	
Nicocles	Sparta	Chariot race (four-horse)
Praxias	[not extant]	Chariot race (four-colt)
Distamenus	[not extant]	Chariot race (two-colt)
Plutades	[not extant]	Horse race (colt)
Apollonius	[not extant]	Chariot race (two-horse)
Habris	Cyme	Horse race
Amyntas	Aeolia	*zeugei diaulon,* "yoked diaulos," apparently a kind of chariot race in which the two horses or mules pulling the chariot ran a diaulos.

[The inscription concludes with the names of three non-athletes.]

Notes: This inscription evokes interest on several counts: (1) It is clear that the athletic meetings at Oropus (if indeed we may assume that this inscription, and the others in the series, do refer to a festival there) did not slavishly follow the Olympic program. Several events not run at Olympia — pentathlon competitions for boys and youth; a far greater variety of equestrian events — were held at Oropus. Likewise, Olympia featured only two competitive divisions, men's and boys', whereas at Oropus, there was the third age group, youth. (2) Not surprisingly, many of the athletes hailed from relatively nearby cities such as Athens and Thebes. The charge is sometimes levelled against the Eleans that their lack of complete fairness in the administration of the Olympic games accounted for the disproportionately large number of Elean athletes who won Olympic crowns. This is surely a groundless complaint; the proximity of an athlete's home to the site of an athletic meeting doubtless was the major factor in his decision to compete in that meeting. (3) The rules at Oropus apparently allowed a boy to compete in the men's division; the case of Leucinas, winner of the boys' boxing and men's pankration, bears this out. (*See also* Aretippus, infra.) Certainly, however, this sort of divisional crossover must have been exceedingly rare.

One final first century inscription from Oropus (*IG* 7.420), after commemorating a large number of musicians and writers, recognizes the athletic excellence of the following:

Name	Place of origin	Event
Metrodorus	Smyrna	Dolichos (men's)
Oulides	Alinda	Stade (boys')
Aretippus	Sparta	Stade (youth's)

Name	Place of origin	Event
Lysas	Myrina	Stade (men's)
Eumenidas	Centuripa (Sicily)	Pentathlon (boys')
Caurinas	Larissa (Thessaly)	Pentathlon (youth's)
Metrodorus	Smyrna	Pentathlon (men's)
Polycrates	Argos	Diaulos (boys')
Aretippus	Sparta	Diaulos (men's)
Eumenidas	Centuripa (Sicily)	Chariot race (two-horse)
Patreas	[not extant]	[not extant]
Philostratus	[not extant]	[not extant]

[Several other names evidently appeared, but the inscription is broken at this point.]

6. The Samian Victor List (Syll³ 1061)

The program of events for what quite clearly was a very localized 2nd century B.C. Samian festival differs significantly from the kind of contests featured at the crown festivals. The heavy events and the pentathlon are represented not at all, although the inscription appears to be incomplete; if so, the missing contests may have been noted elsewhere in the text.

Also listed are several activities — one hestitates to call them contests — apparently not attested elsewhere, at least not at the crown festivals: *euexia* ("good condition"); *eutaxia* ("good order"); *philoponia* ("love of effort"). The unabridged Liddell and Scott Greek lexicon cites this inscription in its entries for all three terms, in each case defining the term as "an event in the competitions [at Samos]." However, the precise meaning of these terms in an athletic context must remain conjectural.

The section pertaining to boys' events (which appears to be complete) includes a number of militaristic exercises not found at Olympia; on the other hand, the pentathlon and the heavy events are omitted. Additionally, competitions were offered in stone-throwing (perhaps a variant of the discus throw, or a kind of shot put).

For none of the winners is a hometown indicated, thus suggesting that all the athletes came from Samos.

The dominant competitor, at least in the youth's events, was Asclepiades; he triumphed in four of the twelve contests.

Boys' events

Event	Winner
Stade race	Demetrius
Diaulos	Aretos
Euexia	Apollonius
Eutaxia	Callidromus
Philoponia	Sopater
Stone throw	Mentor

Events for youth

Event	Winner
Catapult	Asterischus
Javelin throw	Asclepiades
Archery	Asclepiades
Armored fight	Sopater
Armed fight (with shield)	Apollas
Dolichos	Asclepiades
Stade race	Sopater
Diaulos	Porthesilaus
Euexia	Hygemoneus
Eutaxia	Asclepiades
Philoponia	Apollas
Stone throw	Theocritus

7. Roman Chariot Race Horses

Two lengthy inscriptions contain the names of about 200 yoke horses used by two different charioteers, whose names are unfortunately not preserved. The longer of these, *CIL* 6.10056, provides the name of the horse, its color, in some cases its sire, and the number of victories credited to it. In the inscription, the horse names seem to be listed randomly; a chronological order may be indicated, but this is by no means certain. The names have been alphabetized in the lists which follow.

African horses:

Name (translation, if any)	Color	Number of victories
Adsertor (Defender)	russet	12
Adsertor (Defender)	russet	1
Adsertor (Defender)	black	1
Aegyptus (Egypt)	black	4
Arista	brown	5
Armatus (Armed)	black	1
Aunara	brown	1
Barbarus (Wild)	brown	4
Barbarus (Wild)	brown	1
Bubalus (Gazelle)	russet	1
Callidromus (Beautiful Runner)	russet	1
Callinicus (Beautiful Winner)	brown	7
Centaurus (Centaur)	brown	3
Cirratus (Curly)	russet	2
Cirratus (Curly)	russet	2
Cotynus	brown	30
Cotynus	brown	3
Cotynus	brown	1

Name (translation, if any)	Color	Number of victories
Cupido (Cupid)	russet	2
Delicatus (Charming)	brown	15
Delicatus (Charming)	russet	2
Derector	brown	3
Draucus	russet	1
Eminens (Outstanding)	brown	28
Exsoriens (Springing up)	russet	2
Fastidiosus (Haughty)	tan	3
Faustus (Lucky)	not stated	128
Felicissimus (Happiest)	black	1
Felix (Happy)	brown	7
Floridus (Flowery)	russet	4
Floridus (Flowery)	brown	2
Fruendus	not stated	1
Frugifer (Profitable)	brown	1
Gemmula (Little Jewel)	russet	7
Gentilis (Pagan)	russet	2
Hederatus (Ivy Crowned)	brown	1
Hilarus (Cheery)	russet	4
Hilarus (Cheery)	russet	1
Indus (Indian)	black	116
Iuvenis (Youngster)	brown	1
Latro (Thief)	brown	1
Leo (Lion)	not stated	58
Liber (Bold)	brown	1
Licentiosus (Licentious)	russet	11
Lucidus (Shiny)	brown	1
Lucidus (Shiny)	brown	1
Lucidus (Shiny)	brown	1
Lybius	black	1
Maurus (Moorish)	black	10
Murinus (Mousey)	not stated	1
Murra (Myrrh)	russet	21
Murra (Myrrh)	black, brown	1
Nitidus (Bright)	russet	8
Nitidus (Bright)	russet	6
Oceanus (Ocean)	brown	6
Olympus	not stated	152
P. . .[remainder not extant]	not extant	35
Passerinus (Little Sparrow)	black	1
Patronus (Patron)	russet	1
Peculiaris (Extraordinary)	russet	4
Petulans (Impudent)	black	2
Polynicenus (Many Wins)	russet	1
Pompeianus	black	16
Pompeianus	black	3
Pompeianus	brown	1

Name (translation, if any)	Color	Number of victories
Pontifex	brown	11
Praesidium (Fortress)	brown	15
Pugio (Dagger)	brown	3
Pugio (Dagger)	brown	1
Purpurio	black	2
Raptor (Thief)	russet	1
Romanus (Roman)	russet	1
Romulus	brown	1
Saeclarus (Pagan)	brown	6
Sanctus (Sacred)	russet	1
Signifer (Standard Bearer)	russet (?)	16
Superbus (Haughty)	brown	3
Superbus (Haughty)	brown	1
Tiber	russet	2
Tyrrhenus (Tyrrhenian)	tan	3
Tyrrhenus (Tyrrhenian)	tan	1
Valentinus (Strong)	black	5
Valentinus (Strong)	black	4
Valentinus (Strong)	black	1
Valentinus (Strong)	black	1
Vastator (Destroyer)	black	2
Victor (Winner)	russet	2
Victor (Winner)	russet	1
Virilis (Brave)	russet	23
Virilis (Brave)	russet	1
Virilis (Brave)	russet	1

Spanish horses:

Acceptor (Hawk)	brown	1
Acereus	brown	20
Achilles	not stated	21
Amor (Love)	white	10
Callinicus (Beautiful Winner)	white	1
Celtiberus	white	17
Chrysippus	russet	1
Decoratus (Handsome)	russet	1
Domitius	black, white	1
Garrulus (Whinnying)	black, white	1
Gelo	russet	1
Inclytus (Famous)	russet	1
Ingenuus (Noble)	brown	38
Latinus	black, white	4
Licentia (Boldness)	black	1
Lupercus	black, white	1
Marcus	not stated	56
Murinus (Mousey)	dark, spotted (?)	3

Name (translation, if any)	Color	Number of victories
Mysticus (Mystic)	russet	4
Nicolaus	white	1
Nobilis (Noble)	brown	1
Noricus	russet	1
Notatus (Branded)	brown	1
Palladius	brown	1
Palmatus (Palmlike)	gray	1
Paratus (Ready)	white	5
Perdix (Partridge)	russet	1
Phaedrus	black	6
Reburrus (Bristling)	not stated	25
Regalis (Kingly)	brown	1
Romula	russet	2
Siricus	russet	7

A similar list (*CIL* 6.10053) preserves the names of 72 horses. In this list, the place of breeding appears instead of the animal's coloration.

Name (translation, if any)	Origin	Number of victories
Abascantus	Thessaly	20
Advolans (Flyer)	Africa	1
Aegyptus (Egypt)	not extant	1
Aether (Bright Air)	Africa	30
Ajax	Africa	22
Alcimus	not stated	6
Andraemo	Africa	8
Andraemo	Africa	1
Aquila (Eagle)	not extant	not extant
Aquila (Eagle)	not extant	not extant
Aquilinus (Eaglelike)	Africa	1
Aracinthus	not extant	not extant
Aranius (Spider)	Africa	1
Arcas	Aetolia	16
Argus	uncertain	30
Arion	Africa	1
Aster (Star)	not extant	not extant
B...[remainder not extant]	not extant	not extant
Baeticus	Africa	6
Ballista (Missile)	Africa	13
Ballista (Missile)	Africa	8
Barbatus (Bearded)	Africa	1
Cali...[remainder not extant]	not extant	not extant
Callidromus (Beautiful Runner)	Cyrene	1
Callidromus (Beautiful Runner)	not extant	not extant
Camm...[remainder not extant]	Africa	6
Candidus (Shining)	Africa	1

Name (translation, if any)	Origin	Number of victories
Cirratus (Curly)	Africa	1
Cotynus	Africa	1
Cutta	Africa	2
Daedalus	Africa	6
Danaus	not extant	not extant
Delicatus (Charming)	Mauritania	1
Draucus	Africa	1
Dromo (Runner)	Spain	1
Eutonus	Africa	4
Eutonus	Africa	1
Exactus (Precise)	Mauretania	1
Excellens (Excellent)	not extant	not extant
Gaetulus	Africa	6
Glaphyrus	uncertain	10
Helius	Africa	1
Helius	not extant	not extant
Hilarus (Cheery)	Africa	1
Hilarus (Cheery)	Spain	1
Hilarus (Cheery)	not extant	not extant
Hirpinus	uncertain	2
Ingenuus (Noble)	uncertain	28
Innoce	Africa	28
Latinus	not extant	not extant
Lucinus (Light)	Africa	1
Lupus (Wolf)	Spain	22
Lupus (Wolf)	Africa	9
Lupus (Wolf)	Africa	1
Maculosus (Spotted)	Africa	1
Melissa	Africa	1
Memnon	Laconia	14
Menippus	not stated	10
Oss...[remainder not extant]	not extant	not extant
Palmatus (Palmlike)	Africa	2
Palumbis (Dove)	Africa	9
Paratus (Ready)	Africa	1
Pardus (Panther)	Africa	4
Passer (Sparrow)	Thessaly	2
Passer (Sparrow)	Africa	1
Peculiaris (Extraordinary)	not extant	not extant
Pegasus	Africa	1
Pegasus	Africa	1
Pistus	Cyrene	1
Pugio (Dagger)	Africa	2
Pugio (Dagger)	Africa	1
Pyrallis	Africa	4
Rapax (Plundering)	Africa	5
Romanus (Roman)	Gaul	1

Name (translation, if any)	Color	Number of victories
Romulus	Africa	9
Romulus	Africa	9
Romulus	Laconia	5
Sagitta (Arrow)	Africa	18
Sica (Dagger)	Africa	1
Silvanus	Africa	1
Silvanus	not extant	not extant
Spiculus (Dart)	Gaul	9
Thelus	Africa	1
Victor (Winner)	Africa	32
Victor (Winner)	not extant	not extant
Zmaragdus (Emerald)	Africa	1

The following horses are identified as *equi centenarii*, horses which had won 100 or more races:

Ballista (Missile)	Africa
Callidromus (Beautiful Runner)	Africa
Hilarus (Cheery)	Africa
Spiculus (Dart)	not extant

8. Gladiatorial Lists from Pompeii

Two inscriptions discovered in Pompeii contain lists of gladiators. *CIL* 4.2508 pertains to a long and very fragmentary inscription which was apparently an advertisement for an upcoming show. Several pairs of gladiators appear, evidently the matchups for the show; a Thracian paired with a murmillo is the most common combination. The gladiators whose names are reasonably legible:

The Thracian Sempronius v. the *murmillo* Platanus
The Thracian Pugnax v. the *murmillo* Murranus
The *hoplomachus* Cycnus v. the Thracian Atticus
The Thracian Herma v. the *murmillo* Quintus Petillius
The *essedarius* Publius Ostorius v. the *essedarius* Scylax
The Thracian Nodu. . .[remainder not extant] v. the *murmillo* Lucius Petronius
The Thracian Lucius Fabius v. the *murmillo* Astus

CIL 4.1182 contains a similar list:

The *eques* Bebryx v. the *eques* Nobilior
The *secutor* Hippolytus v. the *secutor* Ce[r]atus
The *secutor* Nepinus v. a Thracian, name not extant

9. The Chelidorius List

A marble inscription (*CIL* 6.10046) of uncertain date lists a number of functionaries in a charioteering *familia* under the control of Titus Ateus Capito. The faction is identified as *chelidorius*, "pertaining to swallows." Not surprisingly, the meaning of this term has been debated; some rather fancifully see in it a reference to Domitian's short-lived Purple faction, on the basis of the purple color of certain species of swallows.

Name	Position
Marcus Vipsanius Migio	not stated
Docimus	*vilicus* (steward)
Chrestus	*conditor* (builder; exact application uncertain)
Epaphra	*sellarius* (saddlemaker?)
Menander	*agitator* (driver)*
Apollonius	*agitator*
Cerdo	*agitator*
Licaeus	*agitator*
Helles	*succonditor* (assistant builder)
Publius Quinctius	*primus* ("first"; exact application uncertain)
Hyllus	*medicus* (physician)
Anteros	*tentor* ("holder"; exact application uncertain)
Antiochus	*sutor* (horseshoe maker)
Parnacus	*tentor*
Marcus Vipsanius Calamus	not stated
Marcus Vipsanius Dareus	not stated
Eros	*tentor*
Marcus Vipsanius Faustus	not stated
Hilarus	*auriga* (driver)*
Nicander	*auriga*
Epigonus	*auriga*
Alexander	*auriga*
Nicephorus	*spartor* (meaning uncertain)
Alexio	*morator* (according to lexicographers Lewis and Short, "in the races, [a person] who strove to embarrass and delay the runners for the amusement of the crowd." The application to Roman chariot racing is uncertain.)
[Name not extant]	*viator* (messenger)

Concerning the term auriga: *Two words — agitator and* auriga — *are used for drivers in this inscription; the standard epigraphical term is* agitator. *It is doubtful that the author substituted* auriga *merely for the sake of euphony or variety. Possibly the* aurigae *were less experienced or less successful charioteers.*

10. Gladiatorial Familiae: Venusian Inscriptions

Two inscriptions contain the names of some of the members of gladiatorial *familiae.* The two tablets were both discovered in Venusia, but because of differences in writing styles, they are thought to record the names of two different *familiae.*

CIL 9.465
The gladiator family / of Salvius Capito / lies here:
The *eques* / Mandatus, (slave of) Rabirius 3 >2
The Thracians / Secundus, (slave of) Pompeius 2 >2
Caius Masonius 7> 4
Phileros, (slave of) Domitius 12 >11
Optatus, (slave of) Salvius, a recruit
The *murmillones* / Quintus Cleppius, a recruit
[name not extant] Julius, a recruit
The *retiarius* / [name not extant], a recruit

This inscription illustrates well Juvenal's (11.20) characterization of the gladiatorial milieu as a *miscellanea,* a mixture of types of combatants. For example, four types of gladiators are listed in the extant portion of the inscription. Many of them were slaves; none (with the exception of Optatus) belonged to Capito.

The significance, or meaning, of the numerals has stimulated some debate, but they undoubtedly refer to some combination of matches, victories, or crowns awarded for victories.

Closely akin to this inscription is *CIL* 9.466, a longer document, with more names and classifications than 9.465. The upper portion of the stone has not been recovered. It seems reasonable to assume that it would have borne a fairly close resemblance in form, at least, to the corresponding extant section of 9.465.

CIL 9.466
Oceanus, (slave of) Avilius, a recruit
Sagittarius / Dorus, (slave of) Piso 6 Ɔ 4
Veles / Mycter, (slave of) Ofilius 2
Hoplomachus / Phaeder, (slave of) Avilius, a recruit
Thracians / Donatus, (slave of) Nero 12 Ɔ 8
Hilarius, (slave of) Arruntius 7 Ɔ 5
Aquila, (slave of) Piso 12 Ɔ 6
Quartius, (slave of) Munilius 1
Caius Perpernius, a recruit
Murmillones / Amicus (slave of) Munilius 1
Quintus Fabius 5 Ɔ 3
Eleuther, (slave of) Munilius 1
Caius Memmius 3 Ɔ 2
Anteros, (slave of) Munilius 2
Atlans, (slave of) Donatus 4 Ɔ 1
Essedarius / Inclutus, (slave of) Arruntius 5 Ɔ 2

Samnite / Strabo, (slave of) Donatus 3   2
Retiarius / Caius Clodius 2
Scissor /Marcus Caecilius, a recruit
Gallus / Quintus Granius, a recruit

11. List of Gladiators: CIL 6.631

CIL 6.631 records the names of some 32 gladiators; the inscription is datable to A.D. 177, on the basis of the consular names (L. Aurelius Commodus and M. Plautius Quintillus) which appear at the top of the stone. The gladiators mentioned in the text were divided into four *decuriae* (groups of ten).

Decuria I

Borysthenes, veteran Thracian
Clonius, veteran *hoplomachus*
Callisthenes, veteran Thracian
Zosimus, veteran *essedarius*
Plution, veteran *essedarius*

Pertinax, veteran *retiarius*
Carpophorus, veteran *murmillo*
Crispinus, veteran *murmillo*
Pardus, veteran *provocator*
Miletus, veteran *murmillo*

Decuria II

Vitulus, veteran *murmillo*
Demosthenes, *manicarius**
Felicianus, *retiarius*, recruit
Servandus, *retiarius*, recruit
Juvenis, *murmillo*

Ripanus, *retiarius*, recruit
Silvanus, *retiarius*, recruit
Secundinus, *provocator*, recruit
Eleuther, Thracian, recruit
Pirata, masseur

Decuria III

Barosus, *retiarius*, recruit
Aemilianus, *retiarius*, recruit
Ulpias Euporas
Proshodus, *retiarius*, recruit
Aurelius Felicianus

Aurelius Felix
Zoilus, *paganus**
Flavius Mariscus
Flavius Sanctus
Diodorus, *paganus**

Decuria IV

Aprilis, *paegniarius*
Zosimus, Thracian
[The fourth decuria had two men only.]

*A manicarius *was probably a tailor who specialized in fabricating the arm-coverings *(manicae) *worn by some gladiators.*

*The word *paganus, *which most often means "civilian," here seems to indicate "townsman" or "villager." It is possible that Zoilus and Diodorus were local men who were somehow involved with these gladiators, perhaps as participants.*

Classical Texts Cited

Following is a list of all ancient sources which provided information for the compilation of this book. Specific source citations appear in each biographical entry.

Classical Literary Texts Cited

Aelian. *On Animals* 6.1; *Various Histories* 2.8, 2.24, 2.27, 3.30, 4.15, 8.18, 9.2, 10.2, 10.22, 11.3, 12.22, 12.58

Aeschines. *Against Ctesiphon* 189

Aristophanes. *Acharnians* 215; *Wasps* 1191–1194, 1206, 1383–1386

Arrian. 2.15

Athenaeus. 4.135D, 9.382B, 10.412D, E, F, 10.413A, B, 10.414E, 10.415A, 11.509B, 13.573E, F, 13.578F, 13.596E

Bacchylides. *Ode* 9

Callimachus. *Fragment* 384

Catullus. 55.25

Cicero. *Concerning the Best Kind of Orators* 17; *Concerning the Orator* 2.86; *Letters to his Brother Quintus* 3.4; *Letters to Friends* 10.32; *Tusculan Disputations* 1.46, 4.41, 4.48

Cornelius Nepos. *Lives* (Miltiades) 1.4

Demosthenes. *Concerning the Crown* 319

Dio Cassius. 59.14, 67.14, 73.19, 22, 78.6

Dio Chrysostom. 28.4, 28.5–10, 29, 31.95–97, 31.126, 78.20

Diodorus Siculus. 1.95, 9.15, 11.70, 11.53, 12.5, 12.9, 12.23, 12.29, 12.82, 13.34, 13.68, 13.82, 14.54, 15.14, 15.69, 17.100–101

Diogenes Laertius. 6.43, 8.47

Dionysius of Halicarnassus. 1.71, 7.72, 8.1, 8.77, 9.37, 9.61, 11.1

Eusebius. *Chronology* (columns 195–207) passim

Greek Anthology. 6.135 (attributed to Anacreon); 6.246 (Philodemus or Argentarius); 6.259 (Philippus); 7.692 (Antipater or Philippus); 9.258 (Lucillius); 9.588 (Alcaeus); 11.75 (Lucillius); 11.76 (Lucillius); 11.77 (Lucillius); 11.78 (Lucillius); 11.79 (Lucillius); 11.80 (Lucillius); 11.81 (Lucillius); 11.82 (Nicarchus); 11.86 (Anonymous); 11.316 (Anonymous); 11.344 (Anonymous); 13.5 (Phalaecus); 13.11 (attributed to Simonides); 13.14 (Simonides); 13.15 (Anonymous); 13.16 (Anonymous); 13.19 (Simonides); 16.2 (Simonides); 16.24 (Simonides); 16.25 (Philippus); 16.52 (Philippus); 16.53 (Anonymous); 16.54 (Anonymous)

Aulus Gellius. 15.16

Herodotus. 2.160, 5.47, 5.71, 5.72, 6.103, 6.105, 6.126–131, 8.47, 9.33

Horace. *Epistles* 1.1.4–6; *Satires* 2.7.97

Juvenal. 2.143ff, 4.94–100, 6.82–113, 7.112–114, 8.199–210, 11.20, 13.97–99

Lucian. *Essays in Portraiture Defended* 19; *Herodotus* 8; *How to Write History* 34, 35; *Parliament of the Gods* 12; *A Slip of the Tongue in Greeting* 3; *Toxaris* 59–60

(Ps) Lucian. *In Praise of Demosthenes* 23

Martial. *Concerning Spectacles* 15, 23, 27, 29; *Epigrams* 2.86, 3.95, 4.67, 5.24, 5.25, 6.46, 10.50, 10.53, 10.74, 10.76, 10.100, 11.1

Menander. *Kolax* (scholiastic comment)

Moral Essays. 58F, 347C, 471F, 521B, 675C, 710D, 753E, 811D, E

Pausanias. 1.28.1, 1.44.1, 2.8, 3.8.1–2, 3.11.6, 3.14.3, 3.15.1, 3.15.7, 4.23.4, 10, 4.24.5, Book 5: passim, Book 6: passim, 7.6.5, 7.17.6–7, 7.27.5–6; 7, 8.17.13–14, 8.26.2, 8.26.3–4, 8.40.1–5, 8.45.4, 10.7.7, 10.9.2, 10.34.5

Petronius. 52.3, 71.6

Philostratus. *Life of Apollonius* 4.28; *On Gymnastics:* passim

Philostratus. *Images* 2.6

Phlegon. *(FGH)* 257.1

Photius. 190 [65], 190 [97]

Pindar. *Isthmian Odes:* passim; *Nemean Odes:* passim; *Olympian Odes:* passim; *Pythian Odes:* passim

Plato. *Laws* 8.839E, 8.840A, D; *Protagoras* 316D, 335E–336A; *Republic* 338C

Pliny the Elder. 7.81, 7.83, 7.84, 7.152, 7.186, 8.160, 10.71, 37.54

Plutarch. *Life of Agesilaus* 13, 20; *Life of Aratus* 3; *Life of Cato*

the Elder 5; *Life of Cimon* 10; *Life of Crassus* 8; *Life of Pelopidas* 34; *Life of Romulus* 28; *Life of Solon* 12

Pollux. 4.89

Polybius. 27.9

Quintilian. 1.9, 11.2

Remains of Old Latin. (LCL; Lucilius) Vol. III, pages 56, 58

Seneca. *Letters* 85.4

Sidonius Apollinaris. *To Consentius* 23.317–427

Simonides. *(Greek Lyric)* 2.30, 2.184, 185

Solinus. 1.96, 97

Statius. 6.668f

Strabo. 6.1, 255

Suetonius. *Life of Augustus* 43; *Life of Caesar* 39; *Life of Caligula* 35, 55; *Life of Nero* 12, 30, 47

Theocritus. 2.115, 7.105

Thucydides. 1.126, 3.8, 5.49, 5.50, 8.35

Xenophon. *Agesilaus* 9.6; *Hellenica* 1.1, 1.2, 1.5, 3.2, 4.1

Zenobius. 6.23

Classical Epigraphical and Paleographical Texts Cited

L'Année Epigraphique. 1960 (139); 1971 (179, 263)

Archivo Español Arqueología. 33 (1960), pp. 126, 128, 130, 131

Carmina Latina Epigraphica. 500

Corpus Inscriptionum Latinarum. 2.499, 3.8828, 3.8830, 3.12925, 3.14644, 4.1179, 4.1182. 4.1474. 4.2387, 4.2508, 4.4340, 4.4342, 4.4345, 4.4353, 4.4356, 4.4377, 4.4395, 4.4420, 5.563, 5.3325, 5.3465, 5.3466, 5.3468, 5.4506 5.5933, 6.631, 6.10046, 6.10047, 6.10048, 6.10049, 6.10050, 6.10051, 6.10052, 6.10053, 6.10054, 6.10055, 6.10056, 6.10057, 6.10062, 6.10063, 6.10078, 6.10167, 6.10168, 6.10177, 6.10180, 6.10183, 6.10189, 6.10195, 6.10196, 6.10197, 6.33950, 6.33983, 7.1273, 9.465, 9.466, 10.7297, 10.7364, 11.1070, 12.3323, 12.3324, 12.5696, 32, 13.1997, 14.2884, 15.6250

Inscriptiones Graecae. 2.2326, 7.52, 7.414, 7.416, 7.417, 7.420, 10.1146, 14.1102

Inscriptiones Latinae Selectae. 5278

Iscrizioni Agonistiche Greche. Numbers 8, 10, 11, 13, 15, 16, 17, 19, 21, 23, 25, 37, 44, 46, 51, 59, 63

Papyrus Oxyrhynchus. 13.1607, 20.2082

Sylloge Inscriptionum Graecarum.[3] 314, 1061

Glossary of Places

(Note: Olympia, site of the Olympic games, was not a city or town, but rather a plain in the northwestern Peloponnesus and home to the famous temple of Zeus, as well as the athletic facilities. The closest towns were Elis and Pisa.)

Place	City, region or island	General location
Acharnae	city	Greece, near Athens
Acragas	city	Sicily
Aegina	island	Saronic Gulf, near Corinth
Alexandria	city	Egypt
Andros	island	Cycladic island, southeast of Greece
Antioch	city	Syria
Aquileia	city	northern Italy
Arcadia	region	Greece (Peloponnesus)
Argos	city	Greece (Peloponnesus)
Astypalaea	city, island	southeast of Greece, near Rhodes
Athens	city	Greece
Batavia	region	Germany
Boeotia	region	Greece
Caria	region	southwestern Turkey
Carystus	city	Greece
Caulonia	city	southern Italy
Ceramus	city	Asia Minor
Cilicia	region	southern Turkey
Cleonae	city	Greece (Peloponnesus)
Colophon	city	western Turkey
Corinth	city	Greece (Peloponnesus)
Cos	city, island	Aegean Sea, near Turkey
Crannon	city	Greece
Crete	island	south of Greece
Croton	city	southern Italy
Cyrene	city	North Africa
Dacia	region	north of the Danube River
Delphi	city	Greece
Dyme	city	Greece (Peloponnesus)
Elatea	city	Greece

151

Place	City, region or island	General location
Elis	city	Greece (Peloponnesus)
Epidamnus	city	Greece
Erythrae	city	western Turkey
Germany		approximates the area of modern Germany
Greece		approximates the area of modern Greece
Heraea	city	Greece (Peloponnesus)
Himera	city	Sicily
Laodicea	city	Asia Minor
Leprae	city	Greece (Peloponnesus)
Lusitania	region	western Spain
Macedonia	region	northern Greece
Magnesia	region	Greece
Magnesia†	city	western Turkey
Mantinea	city	Greece (Peloponnesus)
Mauritania	region	North Africa
Megara	city	Greece, near Athens
Menelaus	city	Egypt
Messena*	city	Greece (Peloponnesus)
Messenia*	region	Greece (Peloponnesus)
Miletus	city	southwestern Turkey
Mitylene	city	Lesbos (Aegean island near Turkey)
Mutina	city	northern Italy
Naucratis	city	Egypt
Naxos	city	Sicily
Opus	city	Greece
Patrae	city	Greece (Peloponnesus)
Pellana	city	Greece (Peloponnesus)
Pergamum	city	western Turkey
Pharsalia	region	Greece
Phigalia	city	Greece (Peloponnesus)
Pisa	city	Greece (Peloponnesus)
Rhodes	city, island	Aegean Sea, near Turkey
Rome	city	Italy
Samos	city, island	Aegean Sea, near Turkey
Scotussa	city	Greece
Scythia	region	north of the Black Sea
Sicyon	city	Greece (Peloponnesus, near Corinth)
Sinope	city	south shore of the Black Sea

Messena and Messenia should not be confused with the Sicilian town of Messana.

†*Called Magnesia on the Maeander (River); sometimes called Magnesia on the Lethaeus (River), a tributary of the Maeander.*

Place	City, region or island	General location
Smyrna	city	western Turkey
Sparta	city	Greece (Peloponnesus)
Stratoniceus	city	southwestern Turkey
Stratus	city	Greece
Stymphalus	city	Greece (Peloponnesus)
Sybaris	city	southern Italy
Syracuse	city	Sicily
Syria	region	between Asia Minor and Egypt
Tarentum	city	southern Italy
Tegea	city	Greece (Peloponnesus)
Thasos	city, island	Cycladic island, southeast of Greece
Thebes	city	Greece
Thessaly	region	Greece
Thurii	city	Italy
Tralles Caesarea	city	western Turkey
Tritaea	city	Greece
Tunger	region	Germany
Tuscia	region	central Italy
Western Locri	city	southern Italy
Xanthius	city	southern Turkey

For a complete and annotated discussion of any of these place names, see *A Dictionary of Greek and Roman Geography*, William Smith, editor, London 1878.

Index